RUTHIE, BRETHREN GIRL

An Autobiography
by
Ruth Rogers Stokes

*To Clarence + Edna Grace,
Friends from North Wales,
our home town.
Many Blessings
Ruth Rogers Stokes
Nov. 2002*

WinePress Publishing  *Mukilteo, WA 98275*

Ruthie, Brethren Girl
Copyright © 1996 Ruth Rogers Stokes

Published by WinePress Publishing
PO Box 1406
Mukilteo, WA 98275

Cover by **DENHAM**DESIGN, Everett, WA

Printed in the United States of America.

ISBN 1-883893-60-7

Dedication

I would like to dedicate these writings to my precious children: Gail and Scott.

With God's nudging and patience, I have tried to share my feelings and happenings in my life that were told to me by my parents and friends I made on my journey through life. May God bless you and yours.

Acknowledgements

A special thank-you:

- to Virginia Winfree from North Carolina who deciphered my handwriting and put it into type form.

- to Lucy Negro who proofread my book and encouraged me to have it published.

- to my dear friend Jeanne Pachella who persevered through my readings to her at the end of the day, and made lunch for me so I could keep on writing as thoughts were fresh in my mind.

- to Ron Lutz, my minister, and his wife Ila, who encouraged me to have my story published.

- a great big thank-you to my mentor Peggy Cramer who pushed, probed, and stimulated me to get these writings in order, edited the manuscript, found a publisher, then set up an e-mail address for me on the computer.

Table of Contents

Introduction

I was challenged to do these writings by Rev. J. Lynn Leavenworth, who was the pastor at Ambler Church of the Brethren during the 1980s.

My dear friend Quinella Beisel died October, 1981. She and her husband, Eugene Beisel, were from western Pennsylvania, but had moved down east years before, same as I had. We met through our business and, as a result, became very close friends and also they became Brethren at our church in Ambler through my husband and me. When she died, she was laid to rest at Geistown Cemetery, which was fifteen miles from where I was living. When I knew the arrangements, I called Gene Beisel and said, "Why don't you and the funeral party stop at my home on the way to the cemetery for lunch and freshen up before going the rest of the way." The funeral party consisted of nine people including Pastor Leavenworth.

When they finished eating, Pastor Leavenworth said, "How did you find this place?" (I had a large picture window off the dining room with a view of about twenty miles looking down mountain.) I lived in the Allegheny Mountains. Route 56 went by my entrance which was the main road from the Pennsylvania Turnpike to Johnstown. I told him how I came back to my roots. Gene Beisel said, as he was listening to our conversation, "You don't know the half of the things this lady has done!"

As I was sharing a few things I thought would interest him, he said, "Did you ever think of writing a book?" I said, "I'm not a writer." He said, "Everyone has a story inside of them" and in the same breath said, "When are you coming down to Ambler?" I said, "At Christmas time to visit the kids." He said, "I want the first chapter on my desk when you come." I looked him in the eye and said, "Are you challenging me?" He said, "Yes!"

A couple of days later I was walking through the woods, I was sharing my thoughts with God, came back, got a tablet, and started writing my first chapter. When I came down east for Christmas, my first writings were placed on Lynn Leavenworth's desk. I will never know what he thought of this book — Lynn died in 1988. (Dear Lynn, Thank you for seeing something in me I didn't know was possible. Through your insight I humbled myself to these writings.)

So, my dear children, through trial and error, this is my story.....

Chapter 1

BEGINNINGS

It all started at the foot of the Allegheny Mountains in northwestern Bedford County, Pennsylvania, in an area known locally as "Dunkard Hollow." My father, John Irvin Rogers, was born on a farm on March 24, 1893, the youngest of three boys to Levi Rogers and his second wife, Catherine Walters Rogers. Grandfather Levi was an elder at the Holsinger Church of the Brethren. His father, Gideon Rogers, was also a Brethren Elder, making me the seventh generation born into a Brethren home. Grandfather Levi had a previous marriage — this union had five children. After his wife's death, he married Catherine Walters; my father, John, was the youngest of three sons to this union.

Being the youngest and also son of a Brethren minister, Dad was raised in a strict home. No reading a paper, playing ball, or working on the Sabbath. These worldly things were frowned upon by Grandpa Levi and the predominantly Brethren Community; so Sundays were spent by the young folk taking walks, while the older folks visited neighbors or just sat resting.

Being born on a farm, chores were given to everyone old enough to work. Dad was the youngest, so he stayed with the women until he could lift and carry things. When he was old enough, he would help in the garden. When it came time to pick the crops, Dad would carry baskets for the women. Everything from the garden was canned, dried, or put into crocks for the following winter. Butter was churned and cheese was made; also apple butter would be boiled in the Fall when apples were ready to be picked. Corn would be dried on top of the cast iron woodstove, which had to be heated by wood cut the proper size; there was not much leisure time. (When I ride by this rocky

Holsinger Church of the Brethren in the early 1900s—
Dunkard Hollow, Bedford Co., PA

My Grandpa Levi Rogers wearing a plain black suit (no
lapels)—he was an Elder at the Holsinger Church

10

mountainous piece of property, I wonder how they existed. They didn't have the tools the farmers have today.)

Dad would tell us kids stories about him and the neighbor boys. They would get together and brag about how many acres of hay they baled or wheat they cradled, or ground they tilled, or how many cows they milked in one hour. These things were done by hand or with the meagerest of equipment, but they were very happy. Their days were so busy they didn't have time to pity themselves or fret about trivial things.

Six days of labor and Sunday was the Sabbath, a day of rest with only the necessary chores, such as feeding livestock and milking cows before everyone in the household was getting ready for church — a must, with no questions asked.

Being a minister's son was no easy task. Everyone's eye was on the minister's kids. The sermons were usually two hours long and sometimes longer. If a guest minister was asked to say the prayer, it was done on bended knee, leaning on pew, with knees on the hard wooden floor! (Boy, I wonder how many of us would do this today without bellyaching!)

Being an active young boy, Johnnie Rogers got quite a few pinches, tugs, and stares from two older brothers and Grandmaw Rogers for not sitting still. When church was over, it was home to a delicious cooked dinner, which was always shared with the visiting minister whom Grandpa Levi invited home. This meant more manners and long prayer of thanksgiving for food. As I said earlier, this was the Sabbath and it was acknowledged by these Brethren people to the fullest. (Which to this day is very meaningful to me, although I do not observe it to the extent and eagerness I should. We Brethren have a beautiful heritage if we would only appreciate it.)

Dad had now grown into a young handsome six-foot man, dark brown curly hair, very steely blue eyes, and clean shaven face! With his two older brothers married and starting new families, Dad had many more responsibilities. So, to bring an income to help over the winter months, Dad had a huckster route. This endeavor consisted of crops grown in the garden. He would hitch up his horse and wagon to take his produce over the mountain to townspeople every Friday. This meant getting up around

4:00 o'clock in the morning to load the wagon and get the horse ready to take this long ride up the mountain through the country village of Ogletown, winding up more mountain which is called Babcock Mountain, and finally leveling off on a straight stretch of road leading into the town of Windber, Pennsylvania, which at that time was a prosperous coal mining town.

There was one special stop at a dentist's home at which Dad lingered a little longer, because a young maiden girl worked for this dentist, and did the buying for this family. She was also the housekeeper, babysitter, cleaning girl, and companion to the dentist's wife. This is where my mother, Minnie Etta Mock, enters the picture. Born February 23, 1893, on top of Babcock Mountain on her father Lemon Mock's farm. She was first of five children born to her parents, each of whom had been married previously.

Grandpaw Lemon was married first to a Nancy Rowzer and they had a son and daughter. Then Nancy died from complications due to a third childbirth, and the baby died also. Grandma Susannah Lint, my mother's mother, was married first to a Wirick and had three sons from this union. With the loss of their spouses, Grandpaw Lemon and Susannah Lint Wirick married, and this union produced five more children. My mother, Minnie Mock, being the eldest of this union.

Being the oldest of five children, Mother was a grown woman before her time! She didn't have much time to play, although I remember her telling me Grandpaw Lemon gave her a beautiful bisque jointed doll. He made a cradle out of wooden pieces of crates. Grandmaw Susannah made it a few clothes and blankets. (I have this doll and cradle which will be given to my daughter and she can pass it on down to her girls.)

By the age of ten, Mother was in charge of the whole household. Grandpaw Lemon and Grandmaw Susannah were "mail carriers." This involved getting up very early, picking up mail and sorting it, then delivering it. During the early 1900s their route was rural, with stops few and far between. Mother would get up with them, make breakfast, so they could be on their way. Now her day was starting, helping younger brothers, doing dishes, making beds, cleaning, and getting supper ready for her parents' return. Her brothers had chores to do consisting of cutting wood and feeding livestock. They always had a few cows, chickens, and horses. Mother said Grandpaw always had the nicest horses around. He fed them well, curried them often, and kept their stalls neat and clean. He never beat any of his animals; he was a kind and gentle man. He showed lots of love for his animals.

When Mother was ten years old, a wonderful thing happened. Grandmaw stayed home from delivering mail one day, said she didn't feel well. Next morning a little baby girl was born! Now Mother had a real live doll to dress, diaper, feed, and take care of. Grandmaw went back to delivering mail as soon as she was able. She would breastfeed the baby in the morning before she left for work, put the baby in the cradle, and go on her way. When the baby awakened hours later, Mother would change its diaper and give it a sugar tit to hold it over until Grandmaw returned in the evening. (A sugar tit is a little bit of sugar tied in a piece of white cloth, dipped into water to moisten, and put into the baby's mouth — hopefully to satisfy it until the real thing arrived.)

In their early years, Grandpaw Lemon's and Grandmaw Susanna's children from previous marriages were put out among relatives or neighbors to work. So they all had an early start growing up quickly. In time they all married and had fine families. Some went to other states. (When I was about seven years old, my mother's family had a reunion with all brothers and sisters and most of their families. What a joyous fellowship, renewing old memories.)

Mother was taken out of school at twelve years of age to go to work. Her jobs consisted of housecleaning and cooking for families who needed outside help. She started working for the dentist, Dr. John Bell and family, when she was sixteen years old, and worked for them until she married Dad in 1913.

Grandpaw and Grandmaw Mock were also Brethren, so religion was also a meaningful part of Mother's life. Home, school, and Church were very important parts of the Mock training, same as in Dad's family. Mother told me stories about her Sunday afternoons. After church she and the neighbor girls would

My Grandmaw and Grandpaw Mock on their farm in Ryot, PA

swing on the porch, or take walks hoping some of the young men would come along with their horse and buggies and maybe go for a ride if they were so daring!

Mother was baptized in the creek near Ogletown Church of the Brethren in 1908, when she was fifteen. (Dad was twenty-one when he was baptized, but I will tell you more about that later.)

Even though Dad and Mom lived fifteen miles apart, they didn't really know one another until Dad came to Windber to sell her produce at Dr. Bell's home. Dad said when he saw Mother, he liked the way she looked. He said she was always so neat and clean with a tiny waist and full breasts. She had light brown hair pulled back in a knot!

It was the first week in November, 1913, when Dad stopped at Doc Bell's home to do some bartering. He looked at Mother and said, "Minnie, I will be coming over the mountain one more time before it will probably snow; how about if we get married? I don't think I can wait until next summer to see you again!" (They had dated just a few times before this proposal. Mother met her in-laws just once before they got married.) Mother was quite surprised and said that she would think about it. Dad said, "I'll give you to the end of the month." They were married November 21, 1913.

Mother wore a pale blue silk dress, which was made by her favorite Aunt Junie. (Juniata was her real name, named after the Juniata River.) Dad bought a new dark brown suit for $10 and high-buttoned shoes for $2. They were married in Johnstown by Pastor William Howe in his living room, with Mrs. Howe as their witness. Mother had known the Howes since she was a little girl. (I don't know if he baptized her.) After the ceremony,

Wedding picture (1913) of my parents, John Rogers and Minnie Mock, taken at Windber, PA

the Bells had a dinner for Dad and Mom in their home, which had an air of sadness. Mother would be leaving this home. And these wonderful people, who treated her like a daughter, would have to get a new girl. They had a little boy, Johnnie, whom Mother was with from the day he was born until now. Sometime later, Mrs. Bell told Mother that Johnnie cried for days and would ask, "Where is Minnie?"

After the wedding dinner and sad farewells, the bride and groom left by horse and buggy into a cold November night, riding through mountainside to foothills of Dunkard Hollow to start a new life, new in-laws, new everything!

The honeymoon was spent working. Dad went about his chores, milking, and farming. Mother was busy being taught the ways of this new home she would be sharing with in-laws and a new husband.

Money was something not discussed at this time, as neither one had any savings. Mother had sent her money home to help her family, and Dad put his money into seed and things that would be needed to eke out a living. Clothing was bare necessities only — one pair work shoes, one pair dress shoes (worn only on Sundays or very special occasions.) All Mother's undergarments, petticoats, and camisoles were handmade! Hats were taken apart and redone with bits and pieces of material taken from dresses to complement each outfit, which wasn't too many!

Mother got along very well with her in-laws. They were warm and gentle people. Mother, being a good worker and a take-charge person, never had any words between them. Dad would be out in the barn or in the fields working until lunchtime and then Mom wouldn't see him until supper. Grandpa Rogers was away a lot of times, doing his duties ministering to the sick, preaching funerals, performing marriages, and sometimes would have preaching engagements in other communities and churches, so Dad and Mom's first year went very quickly.

The following November, Mother was expecting her first baby. What an exciting time for her watching the change in her body as she grew larger, anticipating the birth of their first child! Sex was never discussed in Mother's home, so what she learned was from older girls who were married, or occasionally from her precious Aunt Junie! When Mother found out she was pregnant, Aunt Junie was first to know, even before she told her in-laws! Dad was quite happy about this but it meant another mouth to feed and clothe.

On November 12, 1914, John Alvin Rogers was born, my first brother! No hospital, just a midwife and Doctor! Being the first baby, Mother had trouble; it was a breech birth. But when that little bundle was put into her arms, all the pain and anxiety was soon forgotten. They didn't weigh babies in those days, but the doctor judged him to be about five pounds! He had blond hair and blue eyes like his Dad! Mother didn't have any trouble breastfeeding Alvin, so soon he gained weight and grew into a healthy, happy baby. Mother said that was a very cold winter, so everyone was patiently waiting for Spring. Then it would be time to plant the crops and work in the garden getting ready for a new summer, fall, and winter!

The next year, the Rogers family had a great sorrow. Grandpa Levi died July 14, 1915. He was loved by his family and community. There are never words enough to say at a time like that, but everyone shared this great loss with the family. People came from far and near. The funeral service was officiated by elder A. G. Croiswhite, assisted by elder C. B. Smith from Kansas, and home ministers. He was laid to rest at the Old Mock Cemetery, Ryot, Pennsylvania. We have a few family members other than Grandpa Levi buried there. (I have a sister, Flora May Rogers, buried there. But my brothers are buried in different parts of Pennsylvania, due to moving away from this area many years ago!) A few years after Grandpa Levi died, his middle son, George W. Rogers, built a new home on the homestead for his growing family.

Knowing Grandma Catherine would be taken care of, Dad decided to make a new life with his young family in New Ashtola, a country village outside Windber, Pennsylvania. Being raised on a farm, Dad had no training of any kind. When he looked for work, the only thing he could get was a job in the coal mines in Windber. (He disliked this job from the first day he started until he quit. He said he felt so cooped up and was scared they might hit gas pockets or have a cave-in.)

This was also a first in his life — rubbing elbows with ethnic people. He had to work side by side, digging and shoveling coal to be put onto coal cars. These men spoke broken English which was hard for Dad to understand! What an experience for a farm lad! He said the hardest thing to get used to was lunch time; from their lunch kettles these men would take sandwiches which smelled like garlic and onions. Their sandwiches consisted of bread cut in half with meat, cheese, lettuce, hot peppers, garlic, and onions. (Which I suppose is where we get our modern day hoagie or submarine sandwich.) But to a farm boy this was too much to be desired! In time he learned to accept their sandwiches and accents which were Italian, Hungarian, Polish, and Slovak, with a few others thrown in. They were strong and agile.

Dad came home from the mines one evening and, during supper, Mother told him they were expecting another baby! Ernest Glen Rogers was born May 27, 1916. Another towhead with blue eyes, and quite healthy. Brother Alvin was eighteen months old when little Glen came along, so Mother had two babies in diapers.

Being a very fastidious woman, she was up to her elbows in diapers which was literally true because all washing was done by hand. Mother met some of the neighbor women by this time and they would help one another during canning time. Also, the Brethren Church was part of their activities. Dad sang in the choir and also helped teach a Sunday School class.

Remember my telling you earlier, Dad was twenty-one years old before he was baptized. When Dad was in his teens, Grandpa Levi wanted him to be baptized, but Dad said he wasn't ready and did not agree on some of the issues, which Grandpa respected him for at that time. Well, he was quite annoyed about the dress issue which was taking place at church. Dad didn't want anyone to tell him how to dress — no stiff-collared shirt and no coat without lapels (wasn't his cup of tea).

But now, being more involved with church activities, teaching, and singing in the church choir gave him new insights. He was realizing what was necessary to be a whole person. He now started studying the Bible and would get reference books from the minister. He was at peace with himself and finally was baptized February 9, 1914.

World War I was going on in Europe. Then President Woodrow Wilson declared War against Germany on April 2, 1917. He had mixed emotions about our country being involved. He would liked to have joined up, but he had a wife and two small sons, plus the fact the Brethren Church does not believe in taking of lives — we are pacifist. Several of his boyhood friends joined the service and that got him to thinking. Also, he was now maturing into a young man with a lifetime ahead of him, so being a husband and a father was quite enough for him to handle at the time. He became more involved with the family and church affairs.

As a new baptized member of the Church of the Brethren, Dad had responsibilities as a parishioner. Also, decisions had to be made, such as Bible study and tithing — one-tenth of your pay must go to the Lord each week. Could it be done? Yes! And this decision was followed throughout the rest of his life. Even when things were done without, one-tenth was taken out of pay before anything else. (I don't agree with this because I guess I'm not Christian enough to go without certain material things. I'm seventh generation Brethren and, at this time of life, am pretty content to get what I want — family first, and church comes second. Maybe God will get through to me to change my way of thinking in the future.)

Getting back to the issue on the dress code; some of the Elders (but not Grandpa Levi) wanted the men to wear high collars, no lapel, and no tie. The women were to wear prayer cover and plain dresses to the ankles. No printed material. There were enough liberals in the congregation so this heated issue was not passed. (I believe this was one of the first Brethren Churches in the area to comply to modern dress of that day.) Although all women members always wore prayer covering or a hat to cover her head; also, all the women had long hair pulled back or coiled into knots. It was optional for the men of the congregation to wear beards, but all Elders had beards.

Growing up with these Brethren traditions, Dad and Mom had quite a future ahead of them. Could they live the way of the

Bible? They left the security of farm living for smalltown living. They met people of all walks of life who were engaged in many more worldly things than they were ever exposed to. Some of the neighbors were foreign with odd-sounding names to their ears. Mother told the story of the foreign woman in the winter time going out to feed chickens, carrying a bucket of water — with no shoes on and snow on the ground. As her feet got cold, she stepped in the bucket of water awhile and then continued out to the chicken coop. When Mother approached her on this matter, the foreign speaking woman said shoes were for getting dressed up for church or special occasions. (What a sacrifice to pay for being poor.)

We must remember World War I was still going on and families were being torn apart, as men were still being taken into the Army. Mother's brother Dorsey, who was twenty-four years old in 1917, was now part of the service being sent to France. What a sad note for the family as sons, brothers, and sweethearts were sent to a country not too much heard of before. He was gassed, but he managed to live through the ordeal to return home. (Uncle Dorsey lived in Michigan for many years and died in 1985 at age 93. I saw him last at the Mock Family Reunion in 1982. His shoulders were still straight and his mind sharp as a tack.)

Dad was still working in the mines, but disliked it more and more each day. One Sunday in church, he was talking to a Mr. Hitchew and mentioned to him about the mines and said he wished he could get out of them. Mr. Hitchew told him about night classes for carpentry. So Dad enrolled, and went to Carpentry School a couple of nights a week, while changing from a miner to a carpenter. Several months went by and, by word-of-mouth, Dad was asked to serve an apprenticeship with a carpenter contractor. This meant less pay, but it would get him out of the mines.

Again it was a sacrifice and another decision to be made by him and Mother. Mother never gave Dad any opposition on decisions. He was the man of the house. It was her duty to please him at all times. Being raised with that philosophy, it was expected of the female species. (How things have changed!)

20

The economy was still very bad and living in town was no easy task because more things had to be bought at the Company Stores. They had a garden, but nothing like on the farm. Grandpaw and Grandmaw Mock lived on a little farm at the end of Windber, Pennsylvania, so Dad and Mom got eggs, butter, and milk from them, which was a big help.

Dad was now beginning to master the hammer, saw, and ruler and really liked working with his hands. He enjoyed reading blueprints, and putting this knowledge to use by seeing a completed building was a feat in itself and provided self-satisfaction.

At that stage in their lives, Dad didn't have a horse and buggy and no car, so all traveling and going to work was by walking. Sometimes, if Dad had a distance to work, he would walk so far with tool chest and maybe be picked up by someone going that way. Now tools were an important part of the job, so when a certain tool was needed it had to be bought, so again it was a decision to get the tool then do without something else. Again, Mother never opposed his decision. So tools were bought to fill a tool chest which Dad made himself. He was very meticulous with his tools. His saws were always sharp, which was done by himself; his hammer, drills, and bits immaculate. These tools were his mainstay. He never borrowed tools and didn't like to lend his, because of his fastidiousness. He never refused, but would hurt inside each time he did. Few respected the tools as he did. After 70 years, some of his tools are obsolete, but still like new.

How he enjoyed working with his hands. This vocation took him to many places far and near. And this accounted for the many moves that were made in their lifetime. Mother always going along with his decisions, but I'm sure inside she had lots of hurts and disappointments she never shared with Dad. As I said before, he was the man of the household and she obeyed his decisions. Financially they were constantly hurting as so many others, but somehow they managed this meager way of living.

When World War I ended, the economy was very bad, and men were coming home from the War maimed, gassed, and mentally disturbed; not enough work to go around. Dad decided to move back to Dunkard Hollow with Grandma Rogers. The old homestead was being used to its fullest once again, with wife, two young sons, and a new baby on the way. James Leonard Rogers was born January 23, 1920, another towhead with blue eyes, and another boy! As Baby Leonard was placed at Mother's breast, she told the Doctor she guessed she would never have a girl. Three boys! What a challenge; all three healthy normal fellows. Living on the farm, the boys had lots of room to run and play. Also, Dad could see them as future helpers, but poor Mom still had the same tasks and a few more added chores with this growing family and no extra help for her.

At that time Dad and Mother didn't have enough money to pay the Doctor. So he said, "John, why don't you give me some hay for my horse." So Dad threw some hay and corn into the Doctor's buggy. That's how brother Leonard was paid for. When we kids got older, Mother told us this story, so we would tease Leonard and tell him he was only worth a bundle of hay and a pile of corn!

I think this may be the time to inject that none of my brothers had nicknames. Dad and Mom both disliked to hear children called by improper names. My oldest brother's name on his birth certificate is John Alvin so he would not be called Johnnie or John Jr. — they called him Alvin. Brother Glen's certificate is Ernest Glen, but that would mean he would probably be called Ernie — so he was called Glen Ernest. Brother Leonard was James Leonard on his birth certificate, so it would probably mean he would be called Jimmie — so Leonard it was. (What could you do with a name like Ruth Naomi but give up and be called Ruthie — okay because I was the baby of the family — which it was until I was married and then sometimes I was called Ruth.)

Financially things were still bad and there was a flu epidemic which hit quite a few of the rural families including Dad and Mom, but apparently they were young and healthy enough that they both survived, although some of their neighbors and older people in the vicinity were stricken quite severely and died.

Mom and Dad with Alvin and Glen in 1918, at the Levi Rogers
farm just after the flu epidemic

I have a picture of Dad, Mom, and brothers that was taken
at that time by a roving photographer who was wandering
through the countryside, came upon the family in the yard, and
asked if they would pose for a picture. Dad and Mom were so
thin-looking it almost breaks your heart, but the boys were
healthy, robust looking. Apparently the photographer gave them
this picture because I doubt if Dad had any money for such a
trivial thing. They probably gave him a meal. Anyway, I have this
precious picture and it depicts the hardships prevalent at that
time.

Since the economy was not improving and the farm did not
produce enough to keep two families, another move was made
to Scalp Level, Pennsylvania, where Dad got a job building a few
new homes. My sister, Flora May, was born May 19, 1922, at
Scalp Level; now Mother finally had a little girl! How happy Dad
and brothers were to have a baby girl move in. She was a new
toy for the boys and a delight for Mother. Mother could now
make fancy little dresses with her sewing machine, instead of

Dad and Mom with Flora May (who died at age 5), Leonard, Glen, and Alvin

all boys clothes. Flora also was a little towhead with big blue eyes. How she was loved, and was special to her older brothers, and how they protected her.

Now things seemed to be picking up financially, so Dad bought a piece of property on the edge of Windber. (He borrowed money from Grandpaw Mock.) In the evenings and Saturdays, he built his first new home. How happy Mother was to have a home all her own.

Dad never worked on Sundays; that was the Lord's Day, which we were taught to observe and did until we were quite grown.

This move into Windber gave my brothers the advantage of going to a town school and learning about town living. They adjusted quite well and were making friends of foreign-speaking boys and girls. As I said earlier in my writing, Windber was a coal mining town, so there was quite a few different foreign tongues represented. But young children can identify with other children regardless of language. So the boys got along very well with them and also did well in school.

The new homestead had enough acreage to have a nice garden, so Mother was plenty busy with canning, sewing, and home-making. She was quite content. They also were quite close to the Rummel Church of the Brethren, so Sundays were always a time of reverence and sharing dinner with church families and relatives. Dad was very much involved with the church and was doing a lot of Bible studying. He enjoyed conversing with the minister and some of the men who were also Sunday School teachers. He seemed to always be seeking for something he couldn't quite capture. (Mother said she thinks his mind was always working.)

On September 10, 1925, I was born into this happy family. Now Mother had two little girls and three sons and a hard-working husband to care for. Mother said it was a very hot September when I was born. When Dad's brother, Sewell, visited to see his new baby niece, he pitied Mother so badly he went downtown to Windber and bought her an electric fan to keep her a little cooler while she was recuperating.

Living in town now, Dad and family had all the modern conveniences: electric, running hot and cold water, and best of all, no more outside jaunts to the privy. My, how modern they were getting.

Dad built this house at Windber, PA, then lost it in the Depression—I was born here in 1925

Again, carpentry work in this area was getting to a stand-still, and Dad got a job in Pittsburgh. This meant he had to leave Mother and children for a week or two at a time, while he got established and could come and get them. Again, another decision had to be made about the house in Windber. Could they continue the upkeep of it plus pay rent for a new home in Pittsburgh? They would try for a while and see what would happen.

This move was one of the saddest moves they ever made. It seemed everything went wrong. They were in Pittsburgh only a few months when my youngest brother, Leonard, went sledding with his sister, Flora, who was now a beautiful five-year-old girl, when they both fell off a sled. Flora bruised her right side and at that time nothing was thought of it. But a few months later, Mother was bathing her and as she washed over her right side, Flora cried and said it hurt. Mother noticed a lump and when Dad came home, she told him about it. They took her to the Doctor, and he said it felt like a tumor. Well, you can imagine how Dad and Mom felt. The Doctor said she would have to have x-rays. It turned out to be sarcoma, a form of cancer. She would have to be operated on right away. When the operation was completed, the surgeon told Dad and Mom the tumor weighed five pounds and there was nothing more they could do for her. She died. This was a sorrowful time for the family. The first girl born healthy, normal, loveable, now taken away from them. Was this dreaded disease in her little body from birth? Did the sledding accident hasten the growth of the tumor? So many unanswered questions. (I ask, Where was God! Two wonderful people gave love and life to a beautiful child and now she is taken from them. Their first daughter and the brothers' precious little sister gone. How do you answer questions the boys were asking about their sister's death? What a sorrowful time but also a growing time for the family. I'm sure Dad's reasoning was "It's God's will.")

Flora May was brought home to Windber and was laid to rest at the Old Mock Cemetery, Ryot, Pennsylvania. I was learning to talk at this stage of my life and Mother said they had a little white casket for Flora. I was led over to it and said, "What a nice bed my sister has."

Along with this tragedy and all the hurt a family can endure, the building boom was again slowed down. So again Dad moved the family back to Windber to the house he had built, but how much longer he could afford this was soon to be found out.

A lot of soul-searching was being done by Dad at this time. If they stayed in Windber, the boys would probably have to go into the mines when they were old enough to work. This hurt Dad something awful. Did he want this for his sons?

At this provoking time, he was corresponding with his brother-in-law, Gerry Seese, who lived on a farm near Harleysville, in eastern Pennsylvania. Dad was telling him in a letter how bad things were and that he was concerned about raising the boys to be coal miners which he didn't want to happen if he could help it. Well, his brother-in-law wrote and told him to bring the family down to their place. They had half a farmhouse empty. Another soul-searching decision; one that was made readily because of circumstances. October 29, 1929, the Crash — the banks were foreclosing all mortgages, which meant no more lending because they had no money. Dad and thousands of people like him lost everything they owned, which meant their precious home. Now what to do? Decisions! Decisions! If they accepted his brother-in-law's offer, it meant leaving all their church friends and relatives. The boys would have to be taken out of school. Would they ever come back again? They would both be leaving aging parents, brothers and sisters whom they might not see for years. Life sure was complicated, but their lives must continue, and hopefully the right decision would be made with God's guidance. This again was a time of soul-searching and prayer between Dad and Mom. (What faith they both had.)

Mother said this was the first time she opposed Dad in their twelve years of marriage; she did not want to move so far away from her relatives and friends. Also to move in with a family she knew little about. What if Dad couldn't get work; so many unanswered questions.

I haven't said too much about my life at this time because of all the heartache the family was enduring, but I was a complete joy to them according to my Mother and Dad. I helped to fill a void in their lives at this particular time. I became a toy for my three brothers to play with and love. I never knew what it was not to be loved and be part of a loving family. We were always very close. Dad and Mother had such a strong love between them that we as children were caught up in this endearment, all our growing years. What a beautiful heritage.

We were taken to Sunday School and church from birth, so church was an integral part of our lives. (What a sad revelation I discovered while growing up that not all families were blessed with this gift.) Dad read the Scriptures and had prayer every night before we went to bed. Also, all meals were given thanks for before the partaking of them. As each one of us got old enough to read, we were given the opportunity to read a few verses from the Bible, so we were all a part of this meaningful experience. (I would like to inject a little humor at this time about discipline. When my brothers became teenagers and started to fight with one another, Dad would make them read the Bible until they forgot why they were mad at each other. Also, they would have to kiss one another which always wound up with a burst of laughter, forgetting what the disagreement was all about.) I only saw my Dad whip my brothers a few times and I'm sure they needed it because he was a very loving and gentle but stern man. He talked first, if that didn't do the trick, then came the stick.

Now getting back to the big move. It was December 1929, when we as a family said our sad goodbyes to relatives, church friends, and neighbors. I was four years old then and we were moving to a far away place. I remember a large truck being packed with our belongings. Dad had an old "Star" car with glass windows, wooden wheels, and with solid tires. He strapped his carpenter chest onto one side of the running board. My brothers had to get in on the other side. It was winter, so my brothers were wrapped in blankets. Mother and I were in the front seat with my kitten, Trixie, at our feet. We also had blankets wrapped around us. (No heaters in cars in those days.) Dad had a big heavy overcoat and gloves. He also had a dress pair of black shoes on with a pair of grey spats over them. He wore spats for years, even when they went out of style.

Dad, Mom, & me "little Ruthie";
this features Dad in his beloved spats

I remember the truck pulling away and us behind it. I remember tears running down Mother's cheeks, but I didn't understand why. It was a long ride, with several stops for gas and toilet breaks. Mother said I slept most of the way.

Chapter 2

THE LONG MOVE—
LEAVING OUR ROOTS

Our new home was on a big farm (located on what is now Ruth Road) near Harleysville, Montgomery County, Pennsylvania. Gerry Seese, Dad's brother-in-law, had moved to that area years before. He was born in the Bedford County area but realized that farming in the vicinity was exceptionally hard because of rocks and hills, so he made the move to Harleysville. Also, the Indian Creek Church of the Brethren was just a few miles from his farm.

The Harleysville area was a farming territory and is in the midst of a predominantly Mennonite Community. We as a family had difficulty adapting to their Pennsylvania Dutch accents, as they did with our coal-mining tongue. What a challenge we had in this new environment. They found it difficult to accept us as we were the foreigners. This was particularly true with the children. We all underwent a great deal of teasing. It was also hard for Mom and Dad to be accepted by these new neighbors; but as they learned to know us, the barriers were quickly broken, especially when they became aware of our religious convictions and moral beliefs. Our beliefs were much alike. They opened their homes to us and friendships were made in spite of our early beginnings.

The boys were enrolled in a one room country school. Remember they came from a town school with lots of classrooms. Now, the first to eighth grades were all in one room. This was quite an adjustment for them to make, plus getting used to the Dutch accents.

We were living on a farm, which Dad and the boys helped maintain, but this couldn't be continued because a farm only produces so much. The Seese children were maturing into young men and women, so they wanted to start families of their own. (In fact when the oldest Seese girl, Rachael, was being courted by her boyfriend, Luke Moyer, whom she later married, I would answer the door when he came to visit her, and I would get the first piece of candy from the box of his gift to her. This has been a joke between us for years.)

At that time, Dad was learning to know the neighbors and heard of a position as a tenant farmer who was needed in the area. Again, a decision was to be made on another move. It turned out to be a godsend, as this gave our family a chance to be independent again.

Mother once again had a home all her own to clean, polish, and decorate for her own little family. My earliest recollection of the people who owned this farm was seeing the lady dressed in furs, wearing lots of jewelry, and smoking cigarettes. My Brethren mother found this highly offensive and, as a result, could never become close to this woman. This was my first awareness of social differences with reasonably wealthy people. The big car, fancy attire, jewelry, cigarettes, and cocktail parties — all of which were completely absent to our background.

Dad had the full responsibility of the farm, so he and the boys were quite busy. They had crops to plant and harvest, cows to be milked, horses to be curried, and stalls to be cleaned. No time for tomfoolery and play.

Things were going quite well when my brother, Leonard (who was ten years old at the time), developed a very severe earache. First, it seemed to be a mild case of just plain old earache. (Before I forget, my Dad smoked a pipe and chewed tobacco, which he had started to do when he worked in the mines and continued these vices until he died.) The blowing of smoke into Leonard's ear didn't help, as he became violently ill, crying with extreme pain, and holding his hands to his ears. (The reason Dad blew smoke into his ears goes back to the old ways of his time. We later learned this procedure was effective in mild earaches as the warm breath, not the smoke, created some relief.)

At that point, Leonard was delirious and a Doctor had to be called in. He had a very high fever and was floundering all over the bed. He didn't know what he was doing. The Doctor said he had a bealed ear (an old expression for a festering inflammation, such as a boil). If he could get his temperature down, he could stop him from convulsing and prevent brain damage. Again, Dad and Mom's prayers were answered. Leonard got better but had to stay in bed several weeks. No penicillin was heard of in those days, so the infection took longer to run its course. (Years later, Mother said he probably had mastoids but the Doctor didn't know enough about it to diagnose it as such.) Whenever Leonard got colds later in life, they always went to his ear.

We were a very fortunate family as far as health went. We kids were rarely sick — only the regular childhood diseases such as whooping cough, mumps, chicken pox, and measles, which the boys brought home from school. (Believe it or not, I never got any of these until my brothers were grown. My first baby disease was whooping cough which I contracted from little Arlene Stuckey, a girl my Mother was babysitting when I was ten years old. A year later I got measles. To this day I never had mumps or chicken pox.)

At five years old, I was quite a healthy tomboy. I followed my Dad and brothers all over the farm. One day Dad and brothers were out in a field cutting hay and Mother gave me a jug of lemonade to carry out to them. Dad said, "Ruthie, I forgot my tobacco, will you run back to the house and get it?" On the return trip with the chewing tobacco, I decided to try some! Tears were running down from my eyes and tobacco juice was dripping from the corner of my mouth; Dad and my brothers saw what had happened. Instead of Dad scolding me, he said to the boys, "I guess Ruthie got too much hay in her eyes and mouth from the wind blowing." (How good Mother's lemonade tasted to my burning mouth. What a lesson!)

At that stage of life I was quite aware of all the interesting things happening on a farm. We always had a pet dog, cat, and rabbits, so I would spend my time playing with these animals. (Mother managed to buy me a few dolls, but I didn't like them very much. I was more interested in balls and bats, and wheels to roll down our graded yard.)

At this time, I'll tell you a story about my precious Mom. My being the only girl, you would think I would spend most of my time in the house with Mother, but I didn't. I would run after my brothers, always trying to keep up with them, no matter what they were doing. Mother decided to get me a wagon so I would have something to play with because I didn't bother with the dolls. This meant she had to get extra money to buy a wagon. She heard about a farmer nearby who needed people to pick strawberries. She worked enough days to buy me a red wagon. My first real toy that meant anything to me. (Aren't Moms wonderful!) Now I had a wagon all my own. I learned to put one leg inside and push with the other, and when I would get going fast, I would run over my foot. I would jump out of the wagon bawling, run into the house to Mother and tell her Leonard pushed me. He was nowhere in sight. (How we learn to protect ourselves at an early age by telling fibs.)

Farm life was quite a good growing experience for us kids. My brothers were learning about animal life and all the care it took to run a farm. (This may explain why none of them followed this vocation when they got older.) We had many good times on this farm. In the winter we skated on the little pond and went tobogganing on a hill near the house. (Dad made two bobsleds and a big wooden wagon for the boys when they lived in Windber and managed to bring them along.) By the way, the skates we used were the kind you fastened on your shoes. Me, being the youngest, my brothers would have to tie them on my shoes. They would stick out about three or four inches past my shoes and I would fall all over the place but still tried to keep up with my brothers. (I never had my own ice skates until I was twelve years old — a Christmas gift from Dad.)

By the way, Christmas wasn't observed in our home with gifts until we moved to North Wales, Pennsylvania. The reason was it was Jesus' birthday, a time of reverence, not a time for frivolous things such as toys. Also, there was still the Great Depression going on, and money was something we didn't have. We were each given an orange and a candy cane. We didn't know any different. We always had a Christmas tree, because I re-

Dad and my three brothers on the Hasser farm

member Dad and the boys going into the woods and bringing back a pine they had cut. Mother, brothers, and I helped to trim it. Our trimmings were all handmade — chains made out of colored construction paper, popcorn made into balls, and objects we kids would make. We didn't have electric lights because we still didn't have electricity at the farm.

At this time I would like to mention I didn't know anything about a Santa Claus until we moved to North Wales when I was eight years old. This part of Christmas was not acknowledged in our home, as I surmise my brothers and I were taught this was Christ's birthday, and it was celebrated as such. Dad was still trying to teach us the ways of the Bible as is revealed in the New Testament.

Dad made no distinction between the races of people as he accepted them all as God's creation. My first experience of a black person occurred at this time. As I mentioned before, we were tenant farmers on Frank and Polly Hasser's farm, and they brought a black man to our farm to help Dad with the farming. He was a huge man, but very gentle and loving. We, as a family, grew very fond of him. My first recollection of him as he got out of the Hasser's car was that he was very different from any man I had ever seen. I walked over and touched his hand to see if the black came off. This huge giant of a man looked down at this little towhead and smiled. Dad and Mom accepted him immedi-

34

ately and reversed the Hasser's orders to feed him on the porch and sleep him in the barn. He ate with us at the table and Mother fixed a room for him on the third floor in the house. This was probably Big Jim's first experience of being accepted as an equal by a white family.

My first Easter Basket was given to me by this black gentleman. Mother always colored eggs and bought us Easter candy which she put on our plates, but we never had Easter Baskets. I also remember telling Mother to leave the kitchen window open, so the Easter Bunny could bring in his eggs.

Dad continued each evening to have Bible reading and now he taught us about the Resurrection, but I was too young at this point to grasp the meaning of it.

At this time I will inject my Dad's viewpoint on the racial subject. When he became a member and a new Deacon of the Church of the Brethren in Ambler, Pennsylvania, he fought tooth and nail with his brother Deacons and Minister as to why they did not have any black members. A large number of black households were within a few blocks of the church.

At that time in my life, I had a very bad experience. Mother had just thrown hot ashes from a coal stove onto the dirt road next to the house. I didn't see her do it. It was summer; I didn't have any shoes on and ran through the hot coals, burning my feet severely. Mother heard me screaming and came running with all her might. She picked me up and carried me inside and put my feet into a bucket of cold water. I got lots of attention for about a week, as I had to be carried around until my feet started to heal. My brothers took turns carrying me. I ate that right up; as I said before, I didn't know what it was not to be loved.

Again we had to move — the Hassers had sold the farm. Dad had first choice at it but, with no money again, had to refuse their generous offer.

Word got around to the neighboring farmers that the Rogers family had to move. By this time, the Mennonite Community was starting to really accept us and a farmer by the name of Derstine saw Dad at the Mainland Country Store. He told him about a small farm that was empty, across the creek from where he lived.

35

The farm was owned by a Mrs. Kase who lived outside Philadelphia. The agreement was that she would pay Dad $10 a month to maintain the house and barn with option to raise animals and raise all our crops from a truck patch. However, she and her bachelor son would like to spend the summers and some weekends in the half of the farmhouse she had furnished for themselves. With no money and still a Depression going on, Dad accepted this offer. So another move was made, from the Seese farm to the Hasser farm and now to the Kase farm, which were all within five or six miles of one another. My brothers were still going to the same one room schoolhouse. This school was called the Metz School. I suppose the property it stood on was once owned by a Metz, and also surmise the Kase farm may have been the Metz homestead at one time.

I didn't go to school the first Fall we lived on the Kase farm because I was too young; but when Mother couldn't find me, I would be in school with the kids. When Mother went to take me home and scold me for running off, the teacher, Miss Ziegler, would say, "Let her stay; she isn't bothering anyone." So I went to school from that time on. (It didn't make me any smarter.)

By 1931, I was six years old and I had to be vaccinated to enroll in school. What an ordeal! (I don't remember going to a doctor in all those six years. As I said before, we kids were very seldom sick.) Now I had to be vaccinated just because the law said so. Boy, what a vaccination! It sure took. My left arm was quite sore and I got feverish and sick to my stomach. I remember the whole family babying me, but I finally got over it and had a scar to show people when they came to visit. Now I knew what it was like growing up. I would be going to school and learn what life was all about.

I haven't said anything about our not going to church in this new vicinity. Dad did not have enough money to pay his one-tenth tithe, or enough money to buy extra gas. We had very few clothes and, as a result, we didn't go. Dad would read the Scriptures on Sunday morning and Mom would lead us in singing their favorite hymns.

We had lived on the Kase farm about a year when we were invited to go to the Indian Creek Church of the Brethren. Sixty years ago this church was very conservative and is somewhat to this day, although they have a piano in the sanctuary now. We went several weeks and, as a result, were visited one Sunday afternoon by the elder and three of his Deacons. I remember seeing this black car driving into our barnyard and these men in their black suits and funny hats getting out of the car. My brothers and I were playing in the yard. I ran into the house and told Dad there were some men outside who wanted to talk to him. We all went into our living room that was used only on special occasions. Apparently, Dad and Mom knew this to be a special occasion. I remember the men taking off their funny flat hats and holding them on their laps.

The elder looked at Dad and said in his Pennsylvania Dutch accent, "Brother Rogers, we notice you and your family have been coming to church and wonder if you would like to become members? If so, would you and Sister Rogers change your mode of dress to ours?" Dad said, "Are you telling us we are not welcome in your house of worship if we continue to wear our present day clothes?" The elder said, "You are welcome if you wear a black suit, no collar or tie, and Sister Rogers wears a prayer covering and plain dress the same as the other women in the Congregation." Dad took the Elder's right hand in his and, looking him straight in the eye, said, "Brother, the Mrs. and I were both born and raised Brethren. We are lifetime Deacons, but if we have to conform to your mode of dress to belong to your fellowship, we will not embarrass you by being present in your house of worship." Awkward goodbyes were made and, as Dad walked them out to the car, he said, "So be it."

What an experience for us kids to see Dad make a stand of his convictions! As a result of this encounter with these Brethren men, we didn't go to church again until we moved to North Wales two years later.

Dad could not get much work carpentering, so he decided to grow a large garden with the boys' help and maybe sell the vegetables in the nearby town. He wasn't the only one with this idea. He and my brothers would fill the car with the vegetables they picked and go into town, but return home with almost as many as they went with because there would be quite a few other people doing the same thing. They would reduce their

Here I am about 6 years old, posing with Dad's prize
watermelons—taken at the Kase farm

prices but to no avail. One day they had a load of watermelons,
which was Dad's specialty at growing. They stopped at quite a
few homes but couldn't sell any, so he told the boys to just give
them away. With tears in his eyes, he told Mother they didn't
even make enough to buy gas.

Dad and Mom were now thirty-eight years old with not much
of a future ahead of them. Dad spent a lot of time with us kids
because there wasn't much else to do. He couldn't afford to buy
any livestock, so we just had a few chickens, ducks, and turkeys
(plus rabbits which we kids made into pets). I must tell you also
that at that time we never knew what it was to be hungry or
cold. We always had plenty of food and a warm house, but we
had very few clothes.

The boys' clothes were handed down to one another as they
grew from one size to another, but I had clothes Mother made
out of odds and ends of her dresses as they wore out. I remember Mother cutting the feet out of her cotton stockings when
they wore out and sewing them up for me to wear. Things never
got any worse financially than they were at that time; it was the
bottom of the ladder. But we survived through it all.

One of our Mennonite neighbors, Leroy Anders and his wife
Mabel, heard about this poor Rogers man not being able to get
work to support his family, and stopped at our farm to see if
Mother and Dad would help them kill chickens and get vegetables ready for them to take to the Farmers' Market in Phila-

delphia. What a godsend! And also, what a long-lasting relationship we had with this warm Mennonite family.

Having three growing teenage boys, our farm was always a hangout for the neighboring farm boys. As a result, Dad decided to keep them out of trouble, so he started them playing baseball. They would choose up sides and play against each other. If they didn't have enough players on one side and I was lucky enough, they would let me play, which gave me abundant training and skill. (When I got older, I became one of the first girls to play semi-pro ball on an all girls baseball team.)

Word got around the neighborhood that every Saturday and Sunday afternoon the Rogers kids were having a good time playing ball and our farm was open to anyone wanting to play. Dad saw this as a meaningful experience for his sons and also for the farm boys. It kept them busy and out of trouble. Our field wasn't big enough to have a regular-size diamond, and Dad expressed this to one of the farmers and, when the farmer saw these boys having such a good time and staying out of trouble, he donated a field to them. With the help of the boys and some of their fathers, they built a backstop and laid out a beautiful professional-size diamond — the first one around. News traveled fast and it wasn't long until these farm lads were being sought after to play other teams. As a result, the first independent baseball team was started outside Harleysville, Pennsylvania — my Dad being the humble organizer of the wonderful friendly game. Thanks to Dad, many good times were had by these country lads.

I was always on the sidelines and when the boys played visiting teams, I was the bat girl. I was now seven years old and quite a tomboy. My brother, Leonard, was five years older than I, so he taught me all about baseball. He would stand me in front of the barn door and would throw the baseball as hard as he could. If I missed it, he would call me a dummy. So I soon caught very well and threw a ball just like a boy. There were some men working on the township road that went by our farm, and every lunch hour they would watch my brothers and me play ball. They couldn't believe a girl could play ball as well as I did. They loved to watch me throw and catch. Dad tried to get a job with them (through WPA) and was refused. Again, he didn't know the right people.

Mrs. Kase was now getting along in years and wanted to sell this wonderful little farm. She asked Dad if he would like to buy it. Again, Dad had no money to purchase this ten acre farm and lovely ten room house. So again a move had to be made. Mrs. Kase didn't push us to move by any certain time, so Dad had time to look elsewhere. The last summer that we lived there, Dad's brother, George, brought Grandma Rogers and Cousin Margaret Rogers (a daughter of Dad's oldest brother, Walter) to visit us. They both stayed a couple of weeks. I remember Grandma walking around the upstairs porch and watching us kids play in the yard. My brothers had a good time teasing their girl cousin and enjoying having a girl their own age to talk with. But on November 10, 1931, Grandma Rogers died — only a few months after her visit with us. And Cousin Margaret died in 1939 (she had TB, which in those days was incurable), a few years after marrying a wonderful fellow and giving birth to a beautiful baby girl. Another young life taken. Why, God?

Again, by word-of-mouth, Dad heard that carpenters were needed in the town of North Wales. Finally Dad could continue his much-loved vocation. He traveled back and forth for awhile and decided it would be cheaper to move into town, as most of the jobs were in nearby communities. So again a decision was made to leave our country way of life for town living.

Before I forget, I would like to inject at this time about my precious brothers, Alvin and Glen. Alvin was sixteen and got a job in a factory in Kulpsville, Pennsylvania. He received five dollars a week for this hard work, which kept the family until we moved to North Wales. He then got a job in a hosiery mill in Lansdale.

Glen was thirteen, going on fourteen, when he graduated from the eighth grade of the Metz School with the highest grades any boy ever had, according to Miss Beula Ziegler. She wanted him to continue his schooling, which meant going to Souderton High School. I will never forget this most meaningful visit from her. We all sat around our dining room table, while she displayed Glen's test papers to Dad and Mom. She told them how happy she was to have a student with his abilities in her class and would like to see him go on to high school. Souderton was about five miles away. The tuition was something like five dollars a year, plus the fact he would have to have a ride. There were no school buses in those days. Dad looked at Miss Ziegler with sad eyes and said, "I don't even have five cents to further this boy's education." As she left the room, tears were running down everyone's cheeks. I cried too; it was the thing to do. So an eighth grade education was Glen's highest schooling at that time, but he continued learning on his own. Later in life he made a remarkable stand to become a very well-liked manager in the Clemens Markets.

Chapter 3

NORTH WALES DAYS

On September 10, 1933, when I was eight years old and had started the third grade in the one room Metz School, Dad made the decision to move to the town of North Wales. We moved the second week in December, 1933. I remember the truck, with our furniture and belongings, stopping at this new home at 127 South Third Street. As we pulled up in our car, the neighbors were looking out their windows. The kids were standing on the sidewalks watching as Dad, brothers, and men on the truck were unloading our contents. I heard one of the kids say, "They must have had a store; look at all the canned goods." Mother had quite a few potted plants, so I'm sure our appearance was quite impressionable to these kids. Also our dialect was different from theirs — we now had a "Dutch-and-coal-miner" lingo. And being fresh off the farm, our mode of dress was quite different. I'm sure we were an amazing sight to behold!

In no time, Mother had the house scrubbed clean and our things put into place as we were now about to learn the ways of town living. (My first experience.) Up to that time of my life, I had been very protected by my family; but I was about to learn that town living was quite different.

We lived three houses from the Reading Railroad tracks. What an adjustment to make to the awful, almighty noise of the steam trains. The grinding of the wheels and the startling whistle as the engineer pulled the throttle at every street crossing. What a great change for us; we were used to the quiet life of country living — now this!

As I said, we moved the second week in December so that meant Christmas was just around the corner. We went shopping in the town of Lansdale. As we were walking down Main

Street, this man in a red and white suit, with long white beard, was ringing a bell and saying, "Merry Christmas." My first experience of a Santa Claus. That Christmas was still a meager one for us because Dad had just started his new carpenter job.

For others, December 1933 marked the repeal of Prohibition. The entire Country celebrated this event, except for the devout Christians. At that time of my life, I never saw any alcoholic beverage in our home; but I do remember a neighbor man coming home quite often inebriated. He had a large family to support and, as a result of his drinking, we knew the family was very often hungry. Mother would make a large pot of vegetable soup and take it over to the woman and her children.

To give you an idea of the national economy at that time, here are some figures:

US Economy 1932-1934

Occupations	Average Annual Earnings
Lawyer	$4,000
Doctor	$3,000
College Teacher	$3,000
Dentist	$2,000
Public School Teacher	$1,000
Registered Nurse	$900
Construction Worker	$900
Dress Maker	$800
Priest	$800
Coal Worker	$700
Waitress	$500
Steel Worker	$400
Textile Worker	$400
Hired Farm Hand	$200

Goods & Services	Average Price
Modern Single Home (6 Rooms)	$2,800.00
New Packard	$2,150.00
New Dodge	$595.00
New Pontiac Coupe	$585.00
Grand Piano	$395.00
Bedroom Three-Piece Set	$49.95
Dining Room Set (8 Piece)	$46.50
Gas Stove	$23.95
Vacuum Cleaner	$18.75
Wool Suit (Mens)	$10.50
Wool Rug 9x12	$5.85
Kodak Box Brownie Camera	$2.50
Alarm Clock	$2.00
Trousers	$2.00
Leather Shoes	$1.95
Wool Dress	$1.95
Sled	$1.45
Electric Coffee Percolator	$1.39
Fielders Glove and Ball	$1.25
Dental Filling	$1.00
Fountain Pen	$1.00
Wool Blanket	$1.00
BB Air Rifle	$ .79
Silk Stockings	$ .69
Double Bed Sheets	$ .67
Silk Necktie	$ .55
Toothpaste	$ .25
Shave-and-a-Haircut: Two Bits	$ .25
Gasoline (per gallon)	$ .18
Cigarettes	$ .15

Food Items	Average Price
Sirloin Steak (per pound)	$ .29
Eggs (per dozen)	$ .29
Butter (per pound)	$ .28
Oranges (per dozen)	$ .27
Bacon (per pound)	$ .22

Milk per quart (Glass Jar)	$ .10
Corn Flakes (8 oz. package)	$ .08
Bread (20 oz. loaf)	$ .05
Sugar (per pound)	$ .05
Onions (per pound)	$ .03
Potatoes (per pound)	$ .02

Back on March 4, 1933, President Herbert Hoover had been told the banking system of the United States had collapsed. What a way to end his last day of his presidency. Not quite three-and-a-half years had passed since the Stock Market Crash had plunged the United States and most of the world into the worst economic debacle in Western history. The Metropolitan Life Insurance Company had reported in 1931 that 20,000 people had committed suicide as a result of the Crash.

Will Rogers said, "We are the first nation in the history of the world to go to the poorhouse in an automobile."

But for my family, my oldest brother, Alvin, had gotten a job in the hosiery mill in Lansdale. Glen was now sixteen years old but jobs were not very plentiful. Leonard and I were to be enrolled in school the week after Christmas vacation. January 1934, Mother took me to North Wales Elementary School. I remember having to show the Principal my vaccination scar and Mother giving him my report cards from the Metz School.

My first day of school in North Wales was quite different from anything I had experienced before. This school had quite a few rooms as compared to the one room country school. Each grade had its own room and teacher. Boy, what a change! Twenty-five or thirty kids, all third graders, as opposed to the same amount of kids in the country school — all ages and grades in one room!

I'm sure I made quite an impression my first day in class, with my Dutch-and-coal-miner accent, and my country clothes. I soon learned to know these boys and girls and was quite fascinated with this new school.

I was soon learning the personalities of these children; and they, mine. I was a little shy but was aggressive with my tomboy actions which started me off on the right foot with the boys. I liked the boys better than the girls and still do to this day. (I would rather be in a room full of men than with two or three women. I can identify with men; most women are catty, which I don't like.) Remember I was raised with all boys and a masculine Dad.

There was one girl at that time who seemed to have taken a liking to me. Her name was Adelaide Lukens. We started our friendship in the third grade and are friends to this day. She tells me how I was dressed my first day of school in a red cotton dress. She said all my cotton dresses had red, white, and blue in them; and occasionally, I wore an aqua one. I guess my shoes were pretty much like everyone else's. My hair was parted on the left side with a big ribbon tied into it. I suppose the ribbon matched one of the colors in my dress. I remember telling Mother a few months later that I didn't want ribbons put in my hair; none of the other girls had them. I was learning the ways of town kids — from the mode of dress to the slang of the day.

I have to inject at this time about my dear Mom. She knew we were poor, but her expression was, "We might be poor but we don't have to be dirty." She was always the first woman on the block to have her sparkling wash out on the line Monday morning. Our home was always scrubbed clean. The curtains had to hang just right and the floors sparkling clean. I'll always remember her getting the paint can out the first breath of Spring and painting our steps that went upstairs. Mom and Dad lived in this home 18 years and I bet there were 18 coats of white paint on those steps and woodwork. (By the way, this was the longest Dad and Mom lived in one home.)

We had lived in North Wales about two years when word got around that my Dad knew how to hew out logs. It was a task he had learned as a young boy, living on the farm, cutting down trees to make more room for crops, and also to build buildings on the farm. One day a gentleman came to our door and asked for Mr. Rogers. When the man was asked to come inside, he told Dad he was looking for someone to help restore the log huts at Valley Forge, Pennsylvania (replicas of the ones used by the Continental Army under General George Washington) and also build some new huts, and had been given Dad's name. This gentleman, Mr. Brumbaugh, had been sent by the State of Pennsylvania to restore all the state parks and the Valley Forge Park was top priority. He said that if Dad would consent to undertake the work, he would give him some men and Dad could teach them this procedure. Dad's reply was, "I have a steady job right now but if you can't find anyone else, let me know."

As the months went on, Dad was approached again and it just so happened his job was phasing out and he would have to wait for his contractor to get more work. So he took the job of restoring the log huts at Valley Forge Park. It was a personally rewarding job, but with little pay and the State was very lax in sending paychecks to him and his men. He taught these men how to hew out the logs and fit them into position, but it was time-consuming work. Some of the log huts they worked on were falling over. Others were so badly rotted they had to be torn down and new ones had to be constructed. This was in 1935, and ten log huts were constructed or restored. (I understand that some more restoration work was done in the late 1980s. I am quite elated that my Dad was involved in restoring the huts with his historic and authentic technique, but know in his humble way it was something he had to do.)

My brother, Leonard, was enrolled in high school but hated it. School was just a waste of time to him, especially when Dad wouldn't let him play football. He was rather small but very aggressive and Dad thought he might get hurt. He played baseball but, as soon as he turned 16, he pleaded with Dad to quit school. Dad wanted him to have the opportunity the two other boys didn't have, but Leonard insisted he would rather go to work than go to school. He got a job in the Tritzel Factory, in Lansdale, making cookies. The smell of the sweet ingredients put into the cookies made him very ill; every night when he came home, he almost puked his insides out. So he quit that job and got a spray painting job in West Point, Pennsylvania. He worked there a few years and finally got out of that also because the fumes made him deathly ill. He started to work for a painting contractor, painting in housing projects, and later went into steeple painting, which he continued until his death in 1973.

Over the years, we adjusted to town living and liked it very much. I would like to tell you about Leonard's remark when we moved into that house. The first day he walked all through the house, went to the back yard and said to Mom, "Where are we boys going to pee? There's only one tree in the yard and the neighbors might see us." Mom said, "You crazy kid; you just walked by it." We had a toilet in this house, but still no big bathtub — we continued to bathe in a large galvanized tub, Mom and I first, Dad and boys after us.

We also had a cookstove in the kitchen to heat the house and to cook on. This reminds me how wonderful this stove was to my girl friends and me while we were growing up. We would come in from ice skating or sledding and open the oven door and put our feet inside to get them toasty warm, plus drinking hot chocolate with cookies Mom would give us. Our home was always open to our friends even though it was probably the most modestly furnished, but much love was shared to all. Dad and Mom always encouraged us to bring our friends home. And, as a result, our home was always bursting at the seams with young people, especially boys.

Dad was now working steady. My oldest brother, Alvin, was working in a hosiery mill in Lansdale. Brother Glen got a job in an asbestos mill in Ambler — the Keasbey & Mattison Company; but he didn't work too long because of the loose asbestos floating around. It made him ill. Dad made him quit and a couple of weeks later he got a job in a grocery store in North Wales. This became his vocation the rest of his life. Leonard was a painter. I had progressed to junior high school.

Our family was now starting to reap the bounty of work. We finally could buy new furniture and rugs for our home. Dad could give Mother extra money to buy clothes for herself and me. The brothers had to pay board of $10 a week, which Mother put into the grocery money. We always ate well. Mother was an excellent cook and good baker. She was still baking homemade bread and pies. Dad and brothers always carried their lunch, so this meant four lunches had to be packed every day. We lived only a few blocks from my school, so I came home every day for lunch. Mother was always there. We never knew what it was not to have

Mother in the house when we came home. No matter what time of day or night, she was there. How lucky we were to have such a warm, loving Mom. (I'm sure our homelife helped mold us into what we became later in life. Thank you, God, for our Mother.)

I would like to share with you at this time how we became involved with the Ambler Church of the Brethren. Things were financially getting better for us (and everyone to a certain degree), but remember the country was still in the Depression. One afternoon Mother was sweeping the front steps when these two elderly, lovely ladies stopped at the house and told Mother they heard we were Brethren. They invited us to the Ambler Church of the Brethren. Mother told Dad that evening about the encounter with these ladies. We had not been steady churchgoers since our encounter with the men from the Indian Creek Church of the Brethren. Although Dad would take us to Quakertown Church of the Brethren occasionally, if we had enough gas and the times were okay. Also, Mother and I went to the Methodist Church which was only a block away.

One Saturday Dad told us we were going to Ambler to church the next day. We were warmly greeted by these two old ladies and they introduced our family to the rest of the Congregation. We became a part of this warm church family. Soon Dad and Mom were put in as lifetime Deacons.

These two lovely ladies I was referring to above were sisters and their names were Mrs. Anna (Reiff) Brunner and Mrs. Amanda (Reiff) Kratz. They were responsible for quite a few people being brought into the Ambler Church, due to their warmth and Christian commitment. Mrs. Kratz was a Sunday School teacher and a pillar of our church and was probably responsible for more lives being given to Christ than anyone else in our Congregation, including the minister. She was a Saint!

Although we hadn't gone to church regularly before the encounter with these two ladies, Dad still insisted on reading the Scriptures to us and also giving table graces. This practice would soon diminish as the brothers were put on night shifts, and started to go out at night with their boy friends. They were now growing into young mature men with their own ideas about life. Getting home by a certain time for Scripture reading wasn't part of it. Now our family life was starting to wane from its strong ties with religion. As far as my brothers were concerned, they were too busy learning the worldly ways and enjoying them. So church was not too much indulged in at this time.

Yet, it is interesting to note when they became family men, they brought their new wives and children to church. So I would be prompted to say at this time, our home teaching from our parents was always with us even though we got sidetracked at times. Not one of my brothers became involved with church work, such as teaching or singing in the choir, although they went to church regularly and very seldom missed Communion. I'm sure as their children came along, they felt the responsibility as a parent to give them some insight into a religion. So our parents' insistence, training, and way of life was inbred into us kids after all. Isn't that what life is all about — teaching, loving, and caring?

Chapter 4

HOSPITALS & MORE

When I was twelve years old, my life was starting to get busy with living and getting involved with other people. One of these people was a lovely lady, Betty Tice. She was a registered nurse, and an aunt to Jeanette Wampole who lived next door.

Remember I told you that we kids were never sick except for the regular childhood diseases the boys got, but I didn't. Well, when I was ten years old, I got whooping cough and a year later I got measles. At that time, when these diseases were diagnosed by the family doctor, a quarantine sign had to be put on the front door. This meant no visitors, or at least no one was to visit if they never had this disease. Betty was visiting next door and stopped in to see how I was. Mother told her the doctor found a heart murmur and, when I was over the measles, he wanted to give me a complete check-up. I never got out of breath or complained of pains in my chest, but the doctor told Dad and Mom I definitely had a heart murmur. He would like them to restrict my activities. This lasted about two months; they couldn't hold this active tomboy down. The doctor also disclosed to Dad and Mom that I had enlarged tonsils and, just as soon as school was out, to have them operated on.

Arrangements were made by the doctor, Mom, and Dad to have my tonsils and adenoids taken out. I went into the Elm Terrace Hospital in Lansdale one day, was operated on, and came home the next day. Betty Tice was with me during the operation; then came home with me and stayed all night until the next day. I didn't know at the time her concern for me, but later found out, the doctor wasn't sure if my heart would give them any trouble during the operation, and also whether it might act up when I came home. It didn't. And only a week or two later, I was playing ball again with the neighborhood team.

Betty became a very close and dear friend of our family from this point on. She talked Dad and Mom into giving me guitar lessons and I was soon involved with a group of young people playing in an orchestra. We were taught by Betty Reichenbach, who had a well-known music studio in Lansdale. She played quite a few instruments and taught them as well. I learned quite quickly and it wasn't long until Miss Reichenbach put me in the orchestra with the experienced players. Boy! I took to this group like a duck takes to water, and it wasn't long until she put me with three other students and called us the "Stringlets." We were her pride and joy; she took us all over the place. We played in churches, men's and women's groups, Christmas programs, and finally we were getting so popular she got us an audition with a radio station, W.I.B.G. in Glenside, Pennsylvania. We were

The original "Stringlets" taken about 1938—Shirley Spangenburg (ukelele), Bernice Moyer (Hawaiian guitar), me (Spanish guitar), and Jack Shepherd (banjo)—later, when Bernice left, she was replaced by Doris Bookheimer

warmly accepted and were soon to be one of the most popular groups on "Uncle Jim's Children's Hour."

We played for several years on this radio show, and were soon to have our own fifteen minute broadcast every Tuesday. What an experience for four young people, ages from twelve to fifteen. My partners were Shirley Spangenburg, Bernice Moyer, and Jack Shepherd. When Bernice Moyer left, she was soon replaced by Doris Bookheimer. Bernice lived in Salford Station, which was about twenty miles from Lansdale and, when the weather got bad in the winter, she couldn't get to practice. Sometimes she couldn't make it on time to drive more miles to Glenside; so as a result, she gave up playing with us. I liked her very much and we stayed friends for years.

As a result of us kids playing music together, our parents became friends, and soon we became one big family. When one of us would have a birthday, our parents would have parties for us, so we became quite close. Even to this day Doris and I are very good friends. We were bridesmaids for each other when we were married. We had baby showers for each other when we started having our children.

Miss Reichenbach divided her students into four playing groups, and I was involved with each one; as a result, I was quite popular with the kids. One Saturday morning while Miss Reichenbach was giving me a lesson, she put words in front of me to a song we were playing and asked me to sing along with her. It wasn't long until I was singing solo for the group. How excited I was when she asked me to sing and play with the new cowboy group she put together. We were called the "Rough Riders."

Once a year we gave a recital at the Lansdale High School. It was coordinated with the Evelyn Gussman School of Dance. Tickets were put on sale for two nights of entertainment. People came from far and near and it soon became quite a popular affair. It took quite a bit of practice, but we kids enjoyed every bit of it. I was quite a busy tomboy — going to school, playing in an orchestra, and still finding time to play my favorite sport, baseball.

I continued playing with this orchestra until I was eighteen and then made the decision to play girls softball and baseball, thus putting this wonderful experience behind me. I couldn't combine the two because practice for both overlapped, so I decided to play ball. Also, by then I had graduated from high school and was working full time at S.K.F., in West Point. I will go into that phase of my life in a later chapter.

During wintertime, I ice skated and did a lot of sledding. I was always on the go. I shall never forget my first pair of shoe ice skates. If you remember, I told you we didn't celebrate Christmas with gifts. Well, when we became town people we got caught up with social activities and we kids were becoming aware of other people's practices — Christmas was quite a time of gift-giving for them.

I remember coming home from school telling Dad and Mom about the gifts the kids were talking of getting for Christmas. Dad said, "Is there something special you would like for Christmas?" I said, "Yes, shoe ice skates." He said, "Get your coat." We went to the Daub Hardware Store a few blocks away. As we walked into the store the owner, Mr. Krieble, asked Dad if he could help him. Dad looked at me and said, "Tell the gentleman what you want." I said with an exuberant smile, "A pair of size 5 white shoe ice skates." Boy, what a happy kid! I could finally throw my brother's oversized skates away.

Things were going rather well. Then Dad's trick knee came out of place. He was walking to the grocery store, slipped and fell on a patch of ice. The knee swelled so badly the doctor couldn't put it into place and told Dad he would have to be operated on. This meant the ligaments would have to be cut and tied under the knee cap. Again a decision had to be made — he couldn't work with a leg like that; also, he had no money to pay the hospital for their service. Dr. Olson told Dad it had to be done, "...no ifs, ands, or buts about it." So Dr. Olson made arrangements for him, and he also drove Dad to Chestnut Hill Hospital. The operation was a success, but he told Dad he would probably have a stiff leg!

I remember going to the hospital with Mother. We went by bus; Mother never drove in her lifetime. It was winter and I remember standing at the bus stop waiting for the bus to pick us up. It was so cold we could blow smoke rings with our breath. Mother went to the hospital as often as she could. I think Dad was in the hospital about three weeks until he was discharged.

That type of operation was quite painful in those days. Today it is called "football knee" because a lot of athletes have this problem, and the operation is quite perfected through arthroscopic surgery.

While Dad was in the hospital, the people at the Ambler Church of the Brethren visited him and also gave Mom food and money to help with expenses. Dad couldn't work for quite a while, so this really helped them through this rough time. It also brought us closer to this new church family.

When Dad came home he had to use crutches, but it wasn't long until he threw them away. He would stand at the bottom step and put as much weight on his leg as he could stand. He would push and straighten his knee until the sweat rolled down his face, but he was soon ready to walk on it. Also, he was not stiff-legged. What perseverance! He couldn't have a stiff leg with his profession. He couldn't crawl over roofs and up and down ladders if that leg was stiff.

Chapter 5

THE WAR YEARS

I was thirteen years of age when Dad said, "Ruthie, I think it's time for you to join the church." The minister at that time was Paul M. Robinson, a promising young intellect from Johnstown, Pennsylvania. A graduate of Juniata College, he was attending Princeton University while filling the Ambler pulpit. He went on to become president of Bethany Theological Seminary in Chicago. Brother Robinson made quite a hit with the Ambler Congregation, especially the young people. As a result of his dynamic sermons and warm personality, the Ambler Congregation came to life. A strong youth group was organized and also a church baseball team, which I got to play on when the bench was short a player.

I was enrolled in a Baptismal Class and was baptized with quite a few other girls and boys. I believe it was one of the largest groups ever to be baptized at one time in the Ambler Church.

I would like to reflect at this time that my joining the church was my Father's decision, not mine. Remember, Dad was always the decision-maker to a point, but when it came to the final decision, it was left up to us. As you know, baptism in the Brethren doctrine is not performed until the age of accountability, which could be preteen to adult, depending on the personal spiritual growth of the individual.

I accepted this act of baptism at that time of my life because it was the thing to do. I did not realize at that time what a challenge being a Christian was. I took religion as a matter of fact. Remember I was seventh generation Brethren — I knew nothing else. So I made a promise to God and the Congregation that I would follow Jesus' teaching, not knowing what the future held for me.

I was a happy-go-lucky teenage girl with lots of friends, both girls and boys. As I said before, our home was always open to everyone and my brothers were now bringing their friends to the house quite frequently. This meant I was involved with these boys who were my protectors when I started dating a few years later.

Mother never knew how many she would have for Sunday Dinner, so she always had lots of food on hand. My brothers' friends would often stay all night — just so they could have Mother's home-cooked meals. What a good time I had teasing, telling jokes, and playing my guitar while we all sat around and sang. We still didn't have a lot of money but had a lot of fun over nothing. I remember the boys saying to one another, "I have a quarter in my pocket; how much do you guys have?" They would put a dollar's worth of gas into whoever's car was there and ride around all Sunday afternoon.

My brothers never gave my parents any trouble; they were working, buying their own clothes, and also keeping their own cars in gas and repairs. My dad never gave his car to the boys to run around in. It was his only means of transportation to work and, if it got banged up, he couldn't work. So each boy in time bought his own used car.

I was still playing ball and also playing in Betty Reichenbach's Band, which kept me busy, but then I started learning to play tennis. I watched some men playing tennis at this private club near a girlfriend's home. The Club was at the west end of North Wales. Every time this girl, Margaret Kibblehouse, would invite me to her home, I would watch these men play. One day a tennis ball went over the fence and I ran to get it and threw it back. As I did, this young fellow retrieved the ball and said, "Haven't I seen you here before watching?" I said, "Yes." He said, "Did you ever play tennis?" I said, "No, but I would like to." He invited me inside, gave me a racquet, and told me to go to the other side of the court. I did. He hit several balls to me and I returned them with not too much effort. He told me to get a racquet and practice at home and, when I got better, to return. I was the only girl to play tennis on that court. It was an all men's private club but, when they found out I could play, they would let me practice with them until their court time began. So now I was hooked on tennis! I still play to this day.

I also have to reflect at this time, my parents would not let me go out for any sports in school because of my heart. But I was a cheerleader, plus manager of the hockey team. I would play all the sports in gym class and drive the gym teacher crazy because I wasn't allowed to play on any of the teams. I was a very aggressive player, wiry, and very fast. I was very thin, but agile. It really hurt inside that I couldn't participate in school sports, so I decided to do my own thing in other sports. My parents couldn't hold me down. I never complained about my heart, so what could they do!

When I was sixteen years old, it was the best of times and yet the worst of times. We were emerging from an agonizing Depression, only to be plunged into World War II. We had enjoyed our precious few years of peace and recovery even as the lights were going out in Europe. Those memories lingered while we set about arming and recruiting, getting ready for the long years of war on two fronts. As the war worsened, it came to touch us all. We found random hours of escape at the movies, watching Orsen Wells as "Citizen Kane" or Greer Garson as "Mrs. Miniver." Swing was still King, and we danced whenever we could to some of the greatest hits of the Big Bands.

In 1941, Benny Goodman's Band just hired a young girl singer by the name of Peggy Lee, who made the song "Why Don't You Do Right" and it sold a million copies.

Kay Keyser's College of Musical Knowledge had a popular radio program mixed with music and audience participation; and a whole lot of fun which made easy listening week after week. Keyser's Band also played for dances and made the hit record "Who Wouldn't Love You", which was a four-million-seller!

Harry James, a trumpet player in Benny Goodman's Band, was an exciting soloist who grew in popularity, started his own band with a string section and, with his sweet trumpet sound, went on to stardom with my favorite song "Sleepy Lagoon." Later he auditioned this crooner, Frank Sinatra, hired him, and the rest is show business history.

Starting in 1940, some 700 Citizen's Committees sprang up to debate the wisdom of what seemed to be a drift towards war. The majority were isolationists and most noticeable was the "America First Committee." In six month's time, the "America Firsters" got 60,000 members. Some of these members were prominent people such as Alice Longworth, daughter of former President Teddy Roosevelt; Kathryn Lewis, daughter of Labor Leader John L. Lewis; and Charles A. Lindbergh, the Lone Eagle of 1927. Lindbergh said that they should stop the talk of invasion and he also made the statement that the three groups that were pressing our country into war were the British, the Jewish, and the Roosevelt Administration.

"Warmonger" was a name thrown at Franklin D. Roosevelt and his administration, and a majority in Congress gave the critics a new reason for using the word. Senator Edward R. Burke and Representative James W. Wadsworth brought before Congress the Selective Training and Service Bill, which called for the first peacetime draft in the history of the United States.

Then came December 7, 1941. Dad, Mom, and I had just returned from church. As usual, Dad turned the radio on to get the news. It was 1:00 p.m. and the voice on the radio said that Pearl Harbor was bombed early that morning. That evening President Roosevelt declared war on the Axis Powers.

What a time for us as a family. I had three brothers — all service age. Would they have to go to war? Would we be divided as a family for the first time in our close-knit lives? What a saddened time for us as a family, and also for the whole Country.

With the bombing of Hawaii and the President's Declaration of War, we as a Country would never be the same again. Our loved ones were being sent to strange-sounding names of islands and countries we never heard of before.

As teenagers, we were caught up with the defense of our country by obtaining part-time jobs in factories, which were being turned into defense plants. My first job was at S.K.F. (not the pharmaceutical company, but the Swedish Ballbearing Company) which was brought here by the Government to train us Americans to make ballbearings for bomb sights. I worked three nights a week plus all day Saturday, while I was going to high school. I received $1 an hour — my first earned money. From that first paycheck I got until today, I never asked my parents for money. I was now "Miss Independent."

Having my own money gave me a responsibility I never had before. Could I handle it? Yes! With our growing up without very many material things, I was quite aware of doing without, which molded my thinking into being thrifty. I would put so

Our family sat for this photo about 1942, just before
Glen went into the Service—Mom and Dad are in front,
in back are Alvin, Glen, Leonard, and me

much away every week and what was left would be my spending money. I bought my own clothes, paid for my music lesson, graduation trips, and also bought my own class ring. It made me feel good not to have to ask Dad for any more money.

As I said earlier, the war started in 1941 and I wondered whether any of my brothers would be taken into the service. My oldest brother, Alvin, was working in a gauge plant in Sellersville when the war started. His work was considered government priority, so he was exempted.

Brother Glen was working in a grocery store and brother Leonard was painting. It just happened both boys were called to take their physicals the same day in Philadelphia. Both boys had gotten married a few months before. Leonard and Jenny Ramsey eloped in January, 1942, because she was only twenty years old and her parents wouldn't sign for her. Glen and Esther Landis got married in the Lutheran Church in Lansdale on July 4, 1942. These Rogers boys got their names in the local paper: first, because they were brothers going into the service at the same time; and secondly, their new brides were hanging on to them so hard and furiously they held up the train.

At that stage of the war, when the men were drafted and their number was called, they had to take their physicals and report for duty the same day. This meant they couldn't come home. So these two young brides didn't want to let go of their men. What a sad time for us as a family and yet a happy time. Dad and Mom now had two new daughters-in-law and I had two new sisters-in-law.

My sisters-in-law spent the day of departing of their husbands together and, later on that same day, they were driving past the railroad station in Lansdale. Jenny looked at a train pulling in and saw Leonard standing on the train steps waiting for the train to stop. Leonard didn't pass his physical; the Army doctors found a heart murmur and did not take him. So they were reunited — what a happy couple! Glen passed his physical and was sent to Ft. McClellen, Alabama, in 1942. Alvin was still a bachelor and was living at home, until his marriage to Veron Callahan in 1944.

All the young boys who ran around with my brothers were slowly being drafted too, so our home was beginning to be very quiet on Sunday afternoons. One of the last fellows to be drafted was Eddie Weigner from West Point. I had a terrific crush on him. I was sixteen years old and he was twenty-two. To him I was just a kid but, of all the boys who came to our home, he was my favorite.

I was now starting to date, but I was never boy crazy like a lot of my girlfriends were. I never had any trouble getting dates so, therefore, I just went on my own way. Playing sports gave me more opportunity to meet new boys all the time. Also, playing in the Reichenbach Band, I would meet new boys and girls all the time. I didn't have very many open weekends.

As a family, we now had lots of letters to write to my brother and also to the other boys. We now had a star hanging in our window, telling the whole world that we had a loved one in the service. Letter-writing was the least we could do to keep in touch with our loved ones. When my brother Glen was overseas, Dad had a map of the European Countries and, as the letters came in from Glen, Dad would pinpoint the locations so he could follow him as closely as possible as to his whereabouts. All the letters that were written by the servicemen overseas were censored, so it wasn't always easy to follow him.

June 13, 1944 — my Graduation Day! What an important time of my life. There was still a war going on and lots of our boy classmates were enlisting in the service, while quite a few of my friends and myself, who couldn't afford college, stepped into full-time jobs at the war plants.

I would like to share at this time my first real disappointment in my life. Several years before I graduated, I knew Dad didn't have enough money to send me to college, so when the service recruiters would come around the school to give talks about joining the different services, I became interested in the nursing program the Navy had. Without Dad and Mom knowing it, I took the written test, passed, but when it came to the physical, I didn't pass because of my heart. I pleaded with the girl recruiter that my heart didn't bother me, and if I got a written note from my family doctor would they give me a chance. She said, "I'm sorry, I'm afraid you would be a risk."

I went home and told Dad and Mom about my episode with the recruiter. Dad said, "So be it." I went to my room and bawled like a baby. Was this heart of mine going to interfere with my future now that I'm a young adult full of life, getting ready to take on the world? Is my Christian faith now being tested for the first time since my baptism? Was that part of being a young adult in a troubled world making me a stronger person, to make decisions and really be independent? Time would tell.

As I said, quite a few of us teenagers were working part-time, so when we graduated we stepped into full-time jobs. While we were working part-time at the S.K.F. war plant, our bosses were all older men or "4F-ers" (who were called so due to not passing service physicals). As a result, they got jobs in war plants.

When we started working full-time, we were thrown into working with all classes of people. I was now learning how the other half of the world lived. (It reminds me of Dad's first months in the coal mines.) I was put into this large room with about fifty older women, who had sons, husbands, or sweethearts in the service. Being fresh out of school, young, and rather naive, these women sure broke me in with their crass remarks, jokes, and gestures. I soon knew which ones to talk to and which ones to shy away from. My being raised in an all boy family didn't make me crude or smart with my mouth — Dad would not let the boys tell off-color jokes or stories in front of Mom and me; also no swearing was included in our vocabulary. So as a result, these factory women soon taught me the facts of life and much more. I was never at a loss for words, so soon learned to handle myself as each encounter arose.

After graduating, I was working full-time, making more money than I had ever made before. I gave Dad and Mom $10 a week board. When I was working part-time, they didn't take any money from me because I was keeping myself in clothes and whatever I needed; but now I insisted on sharing my earnings. This gave Mom a chance to buy more things for herself. Dad was working in a plant in North Wales called Luscombe. We were now starting to have an income we never had before. The whole country was working and money was something every family was now starting to have; but a lot of material things could not be bought (such as cars, washing machines, refrigerators, and stoves) because the metals used for making those things were now used to make guns, ammo, artillery, and war equipment.

An enterprise called "Black Marketing" was getting very popular. If you knew the right people (or should I say "shysters") you could buy their product, but for much more money than it was worth. This made these people millionaires while our boys were fighting to keep our country a safe place to live. The soldiers themselves got only a few dollars a month protecting us. Those Black Marketeers were making fortunes. So conscientious people, such as my family, would never enter into this type of endeavor.

War is hell; but at the same time it brought the whole Country together in a loving and understanding way. There was an air of dignity and trust among people never shown before. Also, it was the first time all the churches in the United States, and also the world, were filled to capacity — concerned families sharing and praying for the safe return of their loved ones. (Why does it take a catastrophe to make some people go to church?)

Canteens were started all over the Country to entertain the service boys when they were on leave. My girlfriends and I got involved with the one in Lansdale. Sometimes we were asked to bring sandwiches, tea, or coffee to this hall, but we were mostly interested in dancing with the servicemen. My favorite service was the Navy. I liked the color of the uniforms and also how the pants fit the derriere. The other service uniforms were loose fit about the buttocks and were not as colorful. These servicemen would be brought in by buses. No one was supposed to leave the hall without a pass and, as a result, we were chaperoned very well. I always obeyed these rules but, of course, some didn't. Also, some of these people became lovers and got married. The rest of us went our separate ways, doing a job that we felt at the time was much needed. We also had special boyfriends we were writing to and waiting for them to come home.

Remember these fellows were far away from home, very lonely, and homesick. So it was easy to fall for their line of bull if you were so inclined. I never had any trouble with these fellows. If they got too friendly while dancing, I would tell them to pretend I was their sister! This soon put them in their place. Once in awhile you would get a smart one and he'd say, "I don't have a sister." I would say, "It's too bad, you don't know what you're missing," and move on dancing with another boy.

We were a generation of young people who grew up quite quickly, these four or almost five years of war. We went from a Depression into a War. Some of us became independent, some young brides and grooms, others moving away to other parts of the country. Some homes were saddened by the deaths of loved ones. It was a time of soul-searching and testing of faith. I remember praying every night for the safe return of my brother and all my boy friends.

By now I had an important decision to make. I was dating a boy for two years and he was going into the Navy. I had just turned nineteen years old. He wanted to be engaged and have me wait for him. Realizing I had a whole lifetime ahead of me, I said I would rather wait and see what the future brought for us. Also, if either of us wanted to date other people, we should. He went away with that arrangement.

I knew I was not ready for marriage. Also, I didn't want to make a commitment which might have to be broken if either one or the other got involved with anyone else. This was one of the first decisions that paid off for me. If I were really in love, I would know for sure when he was away. "Absence makes the heart grow fonder" was the expression at that time. As a result, when he came home from boot camp training, I thought I would be thrilled to death to see him, but I wasn't. He had already changed.

This was what happened to so many of the boys. He was being sent overseas, so I couldn't tell him face to face, "I'd like to call it off." I waited until he was in San Diego and sent him a "Dear John" letter. (When is the right time to not intentionally hurt someone you are fond of? The letter was sent and it was finished.) To this day, he is the only boyfriend I am not friendly with. All the other fellows I dated and played sports with are still friends even though we are all married to different spouses. I think that says a lot about friendship. I knew on his first leave I didn't really love him, so why hurt both of us when the truth is the truth. Dad and Mom always taught us kids to be truthful even if it hurt.

I was writing to several other boys in the service. When they started to get too possessive, I would write them, "Hey look, you're a nice guy, but I'm not in love with you. I'll continue writing to you but don't get serious about our relationship." I never led a boy on, to intentionally hurt him. That's why I think I had so many fellows as friends. I understood them and their ways and they respected me for what I was. Would you say my home training was now starting to show?

The War was starting to taper off and everyone was waiting for the end of this hellish involvement to take place. Quite a few of the servicemen who were wounded were now being sent home to hospitals in their area to recuperate. Valley Forge, Pennsylvania, had one of the largest Veterans hospitals in our area; so again my girlfriends and I were involved to entertain these men. Some were blind, some had legs and arms off, and some were mentally disturbed. We would read to them, push them in wheelchairs, and most of all write letters to their families for them. Such a small price for us to pay for those poor boys who gave their bodies for our Country. We soon learned to be compassionate and caring. What an experience for us.

Chapter 6

WORK, SOFTBALL—
AND HARRY

It was the Spring of 1945, and I had just entered the door to work at S.K.F. A Mr. Cassel, the personnel man said, "Ruthie, would you come into my office." He asked me if I would help organize a girls softball team. He said, "I hear by the grapevine that you are quite a ball player." He also said they had just hired a young man to be the Athletic Director and he would like you to work with him in organizing a team. I told him I would think about it. A week later, I looked up from my desk and standing in front of me was Mr. Rosenberger from personnel along with a young gentleman. Mr. Rosenberger said, "Ruthie, I would like you to meet our new Athletic Director, Harry Stokes. I made arrangements for you to have a meeting with us at 2:00 p.m. this afternoon in my office."

As the two men walked away, all the women in the room whistled and made quite a few side remarks. I looked at the girl sitting next to me and said, "Boy, did you see that guy's big brown eyes and pretty skin?"

I went to the meeting at 2:00 p.m. and helped organize the first girls softball team the plant ever had. We had posters put on bulletin boards all through the plant, and also gave an invitation over the P.A. System. We had a good response — the middle of April we had our first tryouts. We had about eighty girls so had to cut fifty. We kept thirty, knowing some of them sooner or later would drop out. At the tryouts Harry said to me, "What position do you play?" I said "Anyone but catch, but I really like to pitch." He watched all us girls try different positions and I was the first girl picked on the team!

S.K.F Girls Softball Team (1945)—Harry was Athletic Director and I am sitting at the right

Now Harry said we would have to "...practice every Wednesday and Friday night and I want everyone here. Our first game will be Friday evening before Memorial weekend at the Lansdale Municipal Park; we will be playing Lansdale Tube. All those who can make it, I want a showing of hands." About half could make it; the rest of us couldn't. Harry came over to me and said, "Why can't you make it?" I said, "I have plans to go to the shore." He said, "Break them; I want you to pitch." I said, "Sorry, I made these plans and I'm keeping them." He said, "Do you have to leave Friday night? Can't you go Saturday morning?" I said, "I'm very sorry; I play in an orchestra and we're playing Friday night and then leaving for the shore." That was our first clash of personalities, but there were more to come.

Needless to say, I went to the shore. The Tuesday after Memorial Day, I received a call over the P.A. System to go to the personnel office. There sat Harry and Mr. Rosenberger. As I walked in, they both stood up and Mr. Rosenberger said, "I see you got sunburned. Did you have a good time at the shore?..." and in the same breath said, "...We lost the game Friday night."

I looked at them both and said, "What are you trying to say, I lost the game because I wasn't there?" I was getting mad. Mr. Rosenberger said, "Harry feels you are an asset to the team and are you going to support it or not?"

Now I had to make a decision about my music. Do I want to continue playing in the orchestra, or do I want to play ball. I couldn't do both at that time. I said, "I'll let you know in a week." That following Saturday morning I took my last guitar lesson. I told Betty Reichenbach she would have to get someone to take my place with the "Stringlets." About the same time the other "Stringlets" had graduated from high school and, as a result, quit playing; so our much beloved "Stringlets" era was put to an end.

I was now free of my music. I was working full-time, playing softball, and having a grand time with my young adult life. We had an interesting first year softball season. We were starting to jell as a team and were learning to know one another. We came in third place, so did not feel too bad about it.

During our second-to-last game of the season, Harry asked me for a date and also would I go to the Softball Banquet which S.K.F. was giving for the team. I said I'd go to the Banquet but wasn't interested in a date. It was only six months prior to this encounter with Harry that I wrote my "Dear John" letter to the sailor, and had made up my mind I didn't want to become involved with anyone as yet. (So I was playing the field, so to speak.) I never wanted for dates. Most of my girlfriends had boy friends in the service, so when they came home on leave, they always had a friend with them. This meant blind dates, which I didn't particularly care for; but I didn't have to see them again if I didn't want to.

At this particular time, a Polish family moved to North Wales. There were two sisters and a handsome, blond brother who was just discharged from the Marines because of shrapnel wounds of the right shoulder and arm. I was introduced to him at the tennis court one evening by my tennis opponent, Louis Sauers. We struck up a conversation and he asked me to teach him to play tennis. He was having therapy on his shoulder and arm; his therapist told him to start slowly with exercise to build it up.

He went swimming and was ready for something more strenuous, so tennis was our game — and also our relationship was firming up. We went to the movies several times and played tennis at least twice a week. After about the third date, Dad said to me, "Ruthie, what is that young fellow's name you were out with last night? I told him. He said, "That's a Polish name." I said, "Yes." Dad said, "That means he's a Catholic." I said, "Yes." Dad said, "He seems like a nice fellow and I notice he has been coming around here quite a bit lately; how do you feel about him?" I said, "I like him a lot." Dad said, "But he's Catholic; what are you going to do about it?"

The next date with this Polish boy was my last one. I knew if I continued to see him, my feelings would get much stronger for him. Also, he was trying to persuade me to give him a commitment, and I knew this little Brethren girl was going to get into a lot of trouble with old Dad, so I broke it off.

You may say, "Then you weren't in love with him or you wouldn't have stopped seeing him." I say, "I know I was getting strong feelings for him and also, if I married him, we would both be hurting our families." His family was very devout Catholic; mine, strong Brethren. Fifty years ago, we respected our parents' beliefs and also I knew that I would have broken my Baptismal vow by leaving my church to marry him. He likewise felt the same, so I stopped seeing him. What honor I had for my parents. (How many young people bother to talk to their parents nowadays about religion and how it will affect them with the person they marry? I'm afraid religion is not an integral part of most young couples' marriages in the 1990s. Was Dad right in asking me to dissolve a relationship which was starting to be meaningful to me?)

Decision-making was now starting to be part of my young adult life. I was involved with all types of people in the work world. My family ties were still very strong. The War was phasing out and happy times were being had all over the world again. As I said earlier, the wounded boys were being sent home and families were now being reunited.

During the summer of 1945, my girl friends, Kitty Wall, Adelaide Lukens, and myself, took our vacation to Ocean City, New Jersey. One day we decided to go over to Atlantic City to walk the longest boardwalk in the world at that time. As we were walking the boards, we heard all kinds of whistles and when we looked up above us, there was a whole bunch of wounded servicemen lined up on a sun deck relaxing at Hadden Hall Hotel. Then I heard a voice say, "You look like Ruth Rogers." It was my sister-in-law Esther's brother, Richard Landis — what a joyous reunion! He was sent to Atlantic City to recuperate until he could be sent home. He had both tendons shot off the back of both knees. He was told he would probably never walk again, but he did quite well. He lived a full life until his death in 1980.

We were out of high school one full year at that time and feeling quite grown up. We all had money of our own and were enjoying the independence it gave us. I was still playing softball for S.K.F.

Remember earlier Harry had asked me to go to the Softball Banquet. So I met him there, sat beside him and when it was over, I was met at the door by another fellow I had made a date with earlier in the week.

Monday morning I was called into the personnel office. There sat Harry looking very disturbed as he looked up at me. He said, "Do you usually run out on your dates?" I said, "No, he was waiting for me at the door." Harry said, "I meant ME." I said, "I didn't know we had a date other than the Banquet." He said, "I thought you took that for granted." I said, "I don't take anything for granted." He said, "I borrowed my Dad's car and wanted to take you to a late movie and then home to meet my parents." He didn't have a car as yet — he had just gotten out of the Navy and hadn't worked long enough to buy a car. So when Dad said he could have his car, it had to be a special occasion. (I was it, and I blew it!) Our second personality clash!

After our first ball practice of the new season, Harry approached me again and said, "Would you like to go out to dinner this coming Saturday night, if you are not busy?" I accepted. Our dinner date didn't impress me too much either, although the General DeKalb Inn had an excellent menu. That was the problem. Harry ordered raw clams on the half shell, which I had never eaten before and wouldn't look at his plate again after the first glimpse. I had shrimp cocktail; they were delicious. My next mistake was to order steak "Well Done" for me; Harry's was "Medium Rare." Well, needless to say, mine wasn't well done; it was "Medium Rare" with the blood running over the plate. Harry said, "Umm, this is just the way I like my steak." I said, "I'm sorry, I can't eat mine like that." He sent it back to be redone but, by that time, my appetite was gone.

The next morning on our way to church Mother said, "That Harry is a nice, clean-looking young man. Is he a Jew?" I said, "I don't know but I'll find out this afternoon; we're going to Green Lane swimming, but I do know one thing, I thought I was out with a cannibal last night when I saw the food he ate."

When Harry came to pick me up that afternoon to take me swimming, I said, "Are you Jewish?" He looked at me, laughed, and said, "My name is STOKES, not STOKESBERG. Why?" I told him Mother thought he looked Jewish. I guess you know if he would have been Jewish that would have been the end of our relationship. (I would have stopped seeing him after that date, with no questions asked but, as Fate had it planned, our lives just started being entwined with each other.)

At that time he didn't ask me to go steady, because I told him I didn't want to be tied down to any one fellow. I was just starting to have a good time being my own "independent self" and no man was going to hold me down just yet. But most of my Saturday nights were being filled with Big League baseball games, wrestling matches, and football games — which Harry happened to have tickets for. He knew I was crazy about sports, so what better way to win this girl's heart. He also was involved in sports all through high school, and won a football scholarship to Gettysburg College only to find out he couldn't go when he graduated because of the War.

August 1945 — we had just started to play a softball game at Bridgeport. We were in our third inning when a lady came running out of her house crying and yelling, "The war is over! The war is over!" We stopped the game, threw our gloves into the air, started hugging and kissing one another, tears running down our cheeks. The people were running out of their houses hollering and shouting, waving the American flag, horns blowing, beer being passed among one another — what a joyous time! That game was never finished!

It took us hours to get home that evening. The streets were jammed with people. Cars were everywhere, tears of joy were on everyone's face: men, women, old and young. By the time I got to North Wales, it was 12:30 a.m. The whole town was surging with people waving flags, hugging and kissing, lights in all the homes, horns blowing, people sharing their feelings about their loved ones who would soon be coming home. During the War, the churches left their doors open all the time so people could go and pray any hour of the day or night. It was also true this night — people were going to church all night long because nobody went to bed.

I remember sitting on our front steps with our neighbors all night. At 6:00 a.m. I went to take a bath and got ready for work by 7:00 a.m. That day at work was a wasted day as far as work was concerned. Lots of people didn't come to work.

Now questions were being asked by the workers, wondering how long the plants would be operating. Also it was a time of change again as the servicemen came home; they would need jobs. There would be some sacrifices made by the working people, plus the heads of businesses all over the United States had to cut down drastically on war production. This meant some of the war plants would be shut down altogether or converted into something else such as automobile plants, refrigerator, stove, furniture, washer and dryer factories.

It was also a proving time for big business to put all their energies into peacetime operations again, giving the American people lots of jobs and money in their pockets. (This made us spend it as fast as it was made which has put us where we are today — in a world of charge accounts and high interest rates that are so overwhelming we can't begin to get it back to normal.)

Some of the departments at S.K.F. were being phased out and, as a result, we young people were let go and the older workers were juggled around and put in other departments until the government closed this plant. We were sent to Personnel to receive our last paychecks and were given a list of factories that were hiring people in the Lansdale, Hatfield, and Ambler area. I chose Dexdale Hosiery Mill in Lansdale because I could get a train to the station and go home by bus, depending on my hours of work.

As I was walking out the personnel office my dear friend, Bill Rosenberger, shook my hand, thanked me for playing softball for S.K.F. and also said, "When we get the final notice to close down this whole plant, we will want people who live locally to help wind up our overall operation. Would you like to be called? It may take three months to six months but, if you are interested, I'll give you a call!" I said, "Okay!"

My job in the hosiery mill started at 6:00 a.m. and I worked until 2:00 p.m. What an experience! I disliked it from the day I started until I quit. The job consisted of sixteen machines — four machines on each side, and an aisle behind with eight more machines. You had to keep all the machines going at all times. There were cones filled with silk which had to be threaded through several gadgets on the machine to keep one continuous thread winding onto a big wooden spool. If this silk thread broke, it had to be tied neatly so as not to make a lump on the spool. My job was to tie these knots neatly and quickly. The girl who taught me was very warm and gentle, but I thought I would never learn this feat. She told me that years before they had tied these knots by hand, but now they had an automatic tie knotter which we fastened around our waist. If the silk broke, you grabbed the two ends and pulled it through this knotter, thereby automatically tying the knot. You also had a pair of sharp scissors in the hand to cut long threads that went beyond knot. I finally learned and was put on my own set of machines.

Coming from a modern war plant to a hosiery mill, which was nothing but a sweat shop, was quite an experience in itself. Working conditions were terrible, no breaks, and just a half-hour for lunch. The bathroom had two toilets, which were filthy, and one grimy sink. It was a rare occasion when I used these facilities. I would wait until I got home.

As I said earlier, it was quite an experience. Most of the girls who worked in this department were very tough and vulgar-mouthed. After a few weeks I was put on my own machines so I didn't have time to talk. As a result, I didn't bother with these girls — they just weren't my type and we had nothing in common. I was told later by one girl I liked that those girls thought

I was "high and mighty" and a snob. I did my job well and I never caused any trouble, so I didn't feel bad about the comment.

It didn't take long to find out which girls the boss favored. He was a short, fat man with brown, curly hair, and with a mouth as vulgar as those girls'. Every Friday was payday. He had a box about a foot-and-a-half long with a strap tied around his shoulders. This box held our pay envelopes. With one hand giving the envelope, the free hand was feeling their busts or bottoms — whichever was the closest. Seeing this routine every Friday, I stood with my whole body in front, facing him, with my scissors held straight at his belly. One Friday as he approached me, I was at my usual stance when he looked at me and said with his Dutch accent, "You think you are hot stuff." And I said, "You lay your filthy hand on me and I'll defend myself." That was that!

Two months later, S.K.F. called me to help close down the plant. I went into Dexdale Hosiery to tell my boss that S.K.F. had called me back, but I'd finish the week out until he got someone to take my place. He gave me a few choice words and said, "For all I care, you could leave now." I said, "Okay, I will." I went back to my machines, got my dress shoes, lunch bag, and sweater. I looked at the running machines. I ran through the aisles and broke every string on each machine and kept on running down the steps to the street.

I ran all the way to the bus station which was about one mile before I stopped running. A bus was waiting to pull out, and I was huffing and puffing as I gave my dime to the driver. As I was reliving those last twenty minutes in my mind, I decided to stop at S.K.F. on my way home and tell Personnel I would start the next day. As I entered the personnel office, there stood my best friends, Mr. Cassel and Bill Rosenberger. I burst into tears and told them what had just happened. They both put their loving arms around me and let me cry my heart out. I told them about that horrible little man. They said they had heard complaints about him from other girls who worked for him. (That was just one of the milestones in my life I encountered, and it also gave me smarts about my fellow man.)

I don't remember if S.K.F. closed at the end of 1945 or beginning of 1946, but I do know I was one of the last people to go. Some of the men were transferred to S.K.F. in Philadelphia, and one of these men was Harry Stokes. He worked several months but didn't like commuting from Norristown into Philadelphia every day. Also, he was involved in a sports program at the Norristown YMCA and some evenings he would get home late, which cut into his sports time.

I would like to inject at this time, the Norristown YMCA didn't have a Director due to the War and, as a result, Harry was being watched by some of the Y Directors. He was approached by two of them in regard to filling this position of Director until they could get a more qualified man. Harry accepted willingly and stepped into this position and gave it his fullest attention for almost a year until a Director was found. He gained a lot of knowledge, plus he was doing what he liked best — advising, teaching, playing, swimming, and meeting new people all the time. He had such a pleasing personality that he captivated everyone who came in contact with him. What a gem! (His personality continued to flourish all through his life. Happy-go-lucky, always helping someone even if it meant his last dime until next payday.) We were now dating regularly, but I still did not want to make a commitment. I still wanted my independence.

After S.K.F. closed, I was off work about two months when I read an ad in the paper about a salesgirl wanted at the Interstate Hosiery Mill in Lansdale to sell hosiery over the counter to customers. I was interviewed and got the job. I liked meeting people, plus I could get dressed up every day. When we were not busy at the counter selling stockings, we would sort the styles, colors, and sizes, and box them, getting them ready to sell. My boss was a little woman from Souderton. She was real sweet but very hyper, and was always afraid she'd do the wrong thing and then get chewed out by the big boss. We all liked her so much, we stood behind her if something went wrong. One day she called me to her desk and said I was wanted in the front office.

When I went into the office, several men were sitting there talking. One got up and introduced me to the other gentlemen. Mr. Greenwalt said, "I have been watching you in the sales department and noticed you are a smart dresser and also very attractive. How would you like to model stockings for us when we bring businessmen in?" I was quite surprised and not prepared for this attention and showed it by my answer, asking, "What do I have to do?" He said, "Wear high heels and you will have to walk back and forth, holding your leg out so the men can see the fit of the stocking. Take your shoes off to show the toe and heel, and show seam so it can be seen. Also show the fit of welt, which is the top of the stocking."

I said that I would do it. It didn't mean any more money, but I did get my stockings free. When I told Dad and Mom about my modeling stockings, Dad said, "How high do you have to pull up your skirt?" I said, "Just above the knee." He said, "Make sure it doesn't go any higher." (Aren't Dads wonderful, always trying to protect their little girls.)

I was now twenty-two years old and quite a well-adjusted young lady. Both of my girl friends, Kitty and Adelaide, were married and each had a little girl. I did not envy them but was happy for them being wives and mothers. I was still too busy just enjoying life, playing tennis, and softball. Harry got me involved with a group of girls from Norristown and I was playing softball several nights a week.

The Fall of my twenty-second birthday, Harry tried to pin me down to a commitment of marriage, but again I gave some thought about his proposal and told him about my heart murmur. If I got married and we both wanted children, maybe I would pass this heart condition onto our children — which I didn't want any part of. We decided that I would get my family doctor, Emil Olson, who knew all about my heart condition, to set up an appointment with a heart specialist at Temple University Hospital in Philadelphia.

I spent one day at Temple with my good friend, Betty Tice the nurse, as my go-between. Five doctors examined me. They put me through all kinds of tests, running, jumping, and breathing. They asked me all kinds of questions. They wondered why I didn't complain of any shortness of breath and also no pains around my heart because of my activities. They told me to wait in the room until they consulted with each other.

Finally this dear little doctor, who was Swedish, took me into his office and told me they could operate on me and repair my damaged heart. I asked what all did it involve and how long would the recuperation be. He said that I would have to rest from nine months to a year, then I would probably be able to continue normal activity. (I guess you can see what I was thinking about — no tennis, no ball, no swimming, no anything for a whole year.) My next question was, "I have a boyfriend who wants to get married; what about having children?" His answer was that I would not pass this heart problem on to my children. He said, "You have a valve that didn't close at birth so, therefore, it is not a disease that would be passed on to your offspring. Yes, you can have children but I would not have more than two. See what the outcome would be with your first birth and space at least two years apart, but I would not have any more. You are a lovely young girl and I am sure your husband-to-be wouldn't want it any other way. We have a heart surgeon here from Boston; I would like him to take a look at you, and then set up a date for the operation." I said, "Wait a minute, I have to think about this. I want to go home and talk to my parents and boyfriend before I make any decisions." (This was a Tuesday and I was to call the hospital by Thursday to let them know my decision.)

Twenty-two years old, with a whole lifetime ahead of me, and now a decision had to be made about my life. I would be the third person this surgeon ever operated on. The other two people he operated on were much older, and they died a few months after the operation — and now he wants me to put my life into his hands!

Decisions, decisions, now how strong is my faith? Also, is my religious background now being put to a test? Again, Dad and Mom said, "It is your decision; you are over twenty-one and whatever you decide, we'll back you." Harry said that he was afraid for me but knew, if I made up my mind to have it done, nothing could stop me. What a soul-searching two days and nights I had until I made up my mind. I relived my whole life over and over again, realizing I had a full twenty-two years of happy, wonderful times with lots more love than a lot of people my age ever had. I had a warm, loving, humble family background and lots of young adult friends. Would God be with me in this traumatic experience I was about to undertake?

The thing that bothered me most was when the surgeon said I would have to rest for about a year. No way could I lie around and not do anything for that length of time. Plus the fact I would lose my job at the hosiery mill and I wouldn't be bringing in any money. The biggest factor was the $5,000 to pay the hospital bill. I knew Dad didn't have that kind of money; also, I couldn't help pay for the bill until I was able to work again, which would probably take me ten years to pay for if I survived. If I didn't survive, Dad would have a hospital bill and a funeral bill to pay. Now, God knows, I had lived this many years without any trouble. Why should I let some surgeon open me up and make me sick when I felt as well as I knew how to feel?

So I'd take my chances with life and wait until they really perfected an operation of this kind, and let the future take care of itself. Thursday morning I called Temple University Hospital and told them to cancel out an open heart operation for Ruth Rogers which was to be performed the following week. What a sigh of relief I got from Dad and Mom (and especially Harry when he called that night to hear my response)! "Now we can get married," he said. I said, "Let's think about it for awhile."

I still didn't want to settle down and, actually, I was afraid if we got married I might get pregnant right away. I wasn't ready for an experience that I knew Harry and I were not ready to handle in our young lives. Again I refused his proposal; I told him if he wanted to date other girls, it was okay with me. Also, I wanted more time before I got tied down. I loved life and was enjoying it to the fullest. Quite a few of my school friends were now married and having families, but that didn't bother me. I wasn't ready for the Diaper Brigade as yet. Knowing how involved with sports Harry was, if I were married and with a baby, I would be sitting home playing little mother, while Harry would be out playing and refereeing, having a good time.

Chapter 7

TWO SURPRISES

By that time our family was growing. Glen and Esther had a little girl, Carol. Leonard and Jenny had two girls and a boy — Barbara, Alan, and Flora May (who Leonard named after our dead sister Flora May). So I had lots of little kids to play with, and enjoyed being an aunt.

Having children was an experience we as a family enjoyed. Dad and Mom were loving grandparents and did quite a bit of babysitting for all occasions. When a new baby was born, Mom was the one who always was called to help with the other children and take care of the house until the new momma was well enough to be on her own. Same way with operations — if a mother with young kids needed an operation, Mom was always there. (What I am trying to portray is we were a close, loving family; that's what life is all about.)

Harry and I were going steady and we were still involved with sports. With the War in the past, jobs were being sought by the returning servicemen. Many had the opportunity to go to college under the G.I. Bill of Rights.

Harry got a job at Frank Jones Sporting Goods Store in Norristown. He was quite happy working with all the sports equipment which was so much a part of his sporting life. Now selling and telling customers how to use all this sports equipment gave him a new horizon to his life and personal growth. He was now doing something he was quite interested in, plus meeting new people and making new friends. (This new job was setting him up for his future vocation which he was unaware of at that time.)

In 1948 Mother was called back to Ryot, Pennsylvania. Grandmaw Mock had a stroke and Mother was summoned to help take care of her. This was the first time in my life Mother was away from our home for such a long time. I had to keep house for Dad and me, which meant cooking, cleaning, washing, and shopping for groceries — a whole new experience.

I would like to inject at this time that it was Summer, 1948, and we still had an icebox. Dad and I had to make sure to put the "ice sign" in the window before we went to work, so our food wouldn't spoil. We left the door open, put the money on top of the icebox, and the ice man would bring in a block of ice, take the money, and leave. That's how things were in those days. We never locked our doors. (How things have changed!) After weeks of Dad's and my "batching" it, Dad said, "Ruthie, let's you and I go to Sears & Roebuck in Norristown and buy Mother a new electric refrigerator. We will surprise her when she comes home from her parents." Boy! What a pleasant revelation of modern technology — a refrigerator — you plug it into an electrical outlet, turn a dial, and the whole insides of this piece of equipment gets cold to prevent food from spoiling. I'm sure we were one of the last people on the block to get a refrigerator, but you must remember we were plain people.

It took Dad a bit longer to accept these modern conveniences and also, maybe the fact he realized Mother always was there to do these menial things, such as taking care of the icebox, plus getting kerosene to fill the cooking stove in summer months, and many more jobs a woman such as our Mom did because she felt it was her duty. Also, Dad was now making more money than he had ever made in his life, so this was one extravagance he splurged on and yet was a necessity that sooner or later would have to be taken care of. As I said earlier, this was the first time in my life Mom was away from us for such a long time. The tables were turned; Mom was away, not Dad, which I'm sure he thought about all the times he left Mom while he took jobs away from home. (I think, deep down in Dad's heart, it was his way of telling Mom how much he missed her and also how much he loved her.)

On Saturday, September 10, 1948, at 11:00 a.m., a big Sears & Roebuck truck pulled up in front of 127 South Third Street, North Wales, Pennsylvania, and delivered a beautiful "Coldspot" refrigerator. After the delivery men left, Dad and I were like two little kids playing with this new gadget. I was emptying the old icebox for the last time, putting all our goodies into the new fridge. It was much larger than the icebox, so it looked empty, but in a couple of days we had it filled. (By the way, this was before a freezing unit was designed.) It was heaven for Dad and me at that stage of the game. I was so happy for Mother to finally have her first modern appliance. (With others coming much later.) Mom never demanded things from Dad and, as a result, she never had a lot of those conveniences until it was almost necessary. She always appreciated what she had and always took good care of them.

That same day, September 10, 1948, at 7:30 p.m., Harry Stokes came to take me out to dinner and, as he was helping me on with my coat, he took a small package out of his pocket, opened it, and placed an engagement ring on my third finger of my left hand!

A few weeks before that, we were shopping and, as we stopped in this jewelry store where Harry knew the owner very well, the owner asked if I would like to look at some rings. I did, and said I liked this particular one. Well, that's the one he placed on my finger.

Dad was sitting in the living room reading when we walked in, and I showed him the ring. He said, "What does this mean; is there soon going to be a wedding?" I said, "Not for another year." Harry said, "Let's make it sooner." But I stuck to my guns. Dad said, "Well, Mother is going to have two surprises when she comes home, a new refrigerator and an engaged daughter."

Harry and I had steady jobs so now we could start planning for the future, and also we thought we both were ready for marriage — I being twenty-three years old, and he, twenty-four. If we didn't know what we wanted now, we never would.

Another month rolled by and on October 11, 1948, Mother called and said Grandmaw Mock had died earlier that morning. Dad and I left the next morning to be with Mother and Grandpaw Mock. My brothers and families would come later to the funeral. This was my first experience of death of a loved elderly family member.

Grandmaw was eighty-four years old, which was a long life. She and Grandpaw Mock were married fifty-seven years, so when

Grandmaw was laid to rest next to her first husband, this was very hard for me to accept. The same procedure would follow when Grandpaw Mock died. He would be buried with his first wife whom he was married to but a few years. According to custom, this was the thing to do. (I didn't think very much of that custom. Here were two people who lived together all those years and at death were separated. I just couldn't accept this. As I got older, I realized death does not mean separation, but how does God justify a reunion between a man and woman who had more than one spouse?)

Grandpaw Mock stayed in Ryot a few months after Grandmaw died, then sold his house, and was encouraged to live with his children, staying with each one a few months at a time. This was the first time he ever did so much traveling. He went with his daughter, Elizabeth, who lived near Cornell University in New York, and then came to stay with Dad and Mom.

Harry set our wedding date for August 27, 1949. I said, "What if that doesn't suit me?" He said, "That's my birthday and it falls on a Saturday, plus the fact I shall always remember our anniversaries." How could I refuse? He always had an answer for everything.

We started saving money for our wedding and were also looking in the paper for apartments for rent. A neighbor, Mrs. Pierce, who lived next to Dad and Mom said she was going to move, and when she paid her next month's rent would ask if the landlord would rent it to Harry and me if we were interested in it.

At that time Harry was living at the YMCA in Norristown. His parents' home had been sold and they moved into an apartment, with one bedroom, so he had to move out — he went to the Y. He was very happy to hear about the rowhouse next door to Mom and Dad. I have to tell you, Harry was very fond of my Mom by now. She was always making him all kinds of goodies which he just polished off at a moment's notice. Also, every Sunday my brothers' families would come home and we would all sit around, playing with the grandkids, while Leonard and I would play our guitars and have a sing-along, which was later followed by a cooked meal by Mom and sisters-in-law. We had a lot of fun over nothing. Of course, Harry and I were being teased at the time by my brothers, who by this time had learned to love

Harry and were accepting him as the last new member of the family.

We rented the house next door and, right away, renovated it to the way we wanted it. Dad, being a carpenter, did all our carpentry work for us, which we really appreciated.

We would work nights and invite all our friends to bring paint brushes and buckets. Mother would supply the food, so we never had trouble getting help. I had been given several bridal showers by girl friends and family, so we were getting our house pretty much in order. After the wedding, we could move into a bright, new, shiny house; and it would be all furnished so we could entertain right away.

Our greatest fun thing in this house was a bathroom Dad built for us in the cellar. The cellar had rather low beams and, in order for the toilet to have the right drainage, Dad had to put a step in front of the toilet. It worked just fine for us girls, but the boys all had bumped heads. This was always a standing joke when new people were introduced to our fun bathroom.

Chapter 8

GIRLS BASEBALL &
A LITTLE GIRL

We were married August 27, 1949, at 2:00 p.m. at the Ambler Church of the Brethren by the Reverend Glen Norris. I wore a two-piece white linen suit, white hat and gloves, and white shoes that laced around my ankles. I didn't want to be married in a gown; I was still too tomboyish and would have felt out of place, so a suit sufficed. Harry had a steel gray suit. His brother, George, was the best man and my best girlfriend, Doris Bookheimer, was my matron of honor. My brothers, Leonard and Glen, were our ushers; and of course Dad gave me away. We had a small reception at home for close friends and family.

We left on a honeymoon to Niagara Falls with a stop off at Aunt Lizzie's home in Cayuga, New York. Grandpaw Mock was staying with her and, when they found out we were going to Canada, asked if we could stop. We had a delightful time with them. They gave us gifts, money, and sandwiches for our next day's jaunt to Canada. It helped defray our expenses. Harry had fifty dollars and I had twenty-five, plus Harry had the title to the car in case it wouldn't make it home. We paid all our bills ahead for one month so when we got settled at home, we could save the next month's bills.

What a super beginning for a young married couple. We had lots of love from our parents, relatives, and friends, so how could we not have a strong marriage? But time would test our relationship and love.

Fourteen days before our wedding Leonard's son, Rodney Rogers, was born. Dad and Mom thought he would be the last

Our wedding photo taken at the Ambler Church of the Brethren—my
Dad and Mom, me and Harry, Nannie and Pop Stokes

grandchild until Harry and I would surprise them with an offspring. But we had too many things we were involved in at that
time, so babies were out of the question. Harry and I were still
involved with sports. He was refereeing and coaching the girls
softball team that I was playing on.

We had been married only a few months when Harry got a
letter from a baseball Commissioner from Allentown, who heard
Harry was managing and coaching a girls softball league. He
wanted to know if he would like to start a girls baseball team
on the East Coast. I was all excited and pushed Harry into a
meeting with this gentleman (I do not remember his name).
We were entertained in his home a few weeks before Christmas, 1949. He told us about the leagues that were already being formed in the Allentown and Harrisburg areas. He would
like to have one around the Philadelphia area and would we be
interested. When he found out I played, he suggested we be a
husband-and-wife team.

Our job was to start the first of the year, 1950, to advertise in papers for girls who were interested in playing BASEBALL, not softball. We would have tryouts at Allentown Airport. If the weather was bad, we could go inside the hanger. Our first tryout was a huge success. We had around 300 girls from all over the state of Pennsylvania. We gave them the opportunity of playing different positions and watched each girl as she was put through different maneuvers. We picked the best players, and later sent them letters of recognition, and invited them for a final tryout.

We wanted only 50 girls. Our goal was to have two teams, 25 on a team. They ranged in age from a 14-year-old to a college graduate who was a physical education teacher. Harry was the coach, and we also had Ralph Moyer for our manager and trainer, and Whitey Clayton who would be an umpire.

We would go to all the big league games in Philadelphia, Baltimore, and New York City, and put on a 3-inning exhibition game before the big leagues started to play. This gave the girls an opportunity to be exposed to crowds of people and also to play under the lights, in case we got the opportunity to play at night. Also, there were always scouts and promoters looking for good girl ball players for their big league all girls baseball teams out West. That was where the first all girls hardball teams originated.

I remember our trip to Yankee Stadium in New York. We were not allowed into the men's locker rooms — so we changed into our uniforms in our cars in the parking lot! After all that, we played 1 1/2 innings when it began to pour rain. What a disappointment, but at least we could say with pride that we "played Yankee Stadium."

What an exciting time for me! I was finally going to play hardball for the first time with an all girls league. Remember I played hardball long before I knew anything about a softball. Now I was getting a chance to put my experience to work. Here I am — a married woman, twenty-five years old — and still playing ball. Dad and brothers were very proud of me, but Mom thought I should be acting more like a lady.

Harry was very supportive and we were photographed and interviewed for both the <u>North Penn Reporter</u> and <u>Norristown</u>

"Norristown Nifties" the girls baseball team Harry
managed from 1950 to 1953—he started this first
girls hardball team on the Eastern Shore

Back Row (L to R): Harry Stokes (manager), Dolores
Osowski, Dolores Szulaski, Ruth Stokes, Erma Keyes, Doris
Heinsbach, Ralph Moyer (trainer)

Middle Row: Skip Scheid, Verna Custer, Joan Scheetz, Gloria
Manetti, Jeanette Penecale, Betty Lou Cassey

Front Row: Joan Douglas, Angie Ermigiotti, Gert Woodland,
Betty Hoy, Mary Jane Robbins, Gail "Gussie" Brown

<u>Times Herald</u> newspapers as the first husband-and-wife to manage and play "big league all girls baseball." Harry got teased quite a bit about having all these women around him and was asked if he could handle them. My answer was, "Yes, I'm the one who gives him the hardest time!"

We made a lot of new friends and also did a lot of entertaining; our home was full of activity. One evening while eating dinner, the phone rang and I answered it. To my surprise I got an invitation to go to Fort Wayne, Indiana, for tryouts for the "Fort Wayne Daisies." I looked at Harry with tears in my eyes and said, "It finally happened. I have been asked to try out for the big leagues and now I will never know if I would have made

NORTH PENN REPORTER, LANSDALE, PA., W

Husband and Wife Talk Baseball

Pictured are Mr. and Mrs. Harry Stokes, North Wales, Mrs. Stokes being a member of the Norristown Nifties, a girls' baseball team which will meet the Lansdale Sons of Italy at Memorial Park tonight. Her husband is president of the Eastern Girls' Baseball League.

Associated Press—International News—United Press

Norristown Times Herald
Montgomery County's Great Home Newspaper

NORRISTOWN, PENNSYLVANIA, SATURDAY, JULY 15, 1950.

CARRY LOCAL COLORS—Proof that baseball is not only for the male athletes, these girls who comprise the Norristown entry in the Eastern Girls Baseball Conference are strictly 'big league' in their own right. Front row, left to right, they are: Mary Jane Robbins, 931 W. Airy St.; Erma Keyes, Frazer, Pa.; Ruth Stokes, North Wales; Verna Custer, Trooper, and Shirley Estock, Center Square. Back row, left to right, are: Doris Heinsbach, Trooper; Joan Scheetz, 216 W. Freedley St., Betty Lou Cassey, 235 W. Fornance St.; Gloria Manetti, Conshohocken; Betty Hoy, 1006 Stanbridge St., and Angie Ermigiotti, Edge Hill. *(Times Herald Photo)*

it or not." (Because I just found out that week that I was pregnant.)

How God works — what timing! If I would have made the big league, it would have put a strain on our marriage. I would have been away from home, nine months out of the year. Even though we felt our love was strong, I'm sure it wouldn't have lasted through all the goodbyes and span of lonely nights. So again, I think God had a hand in our lives for an even greater experience we would encounter in the future. And I continued to play ball locally that whole summer of 1950.

As I said before, we formed two teams. One was called the "Norristown Nifties" (uniforms were blue and red) and the other the "Philadelphia Fillies" (uniforms were gold and green). We really had some excellent ballplayers and it was a joy for me to be part of this team. Most of the girls who were on the "Fillies" team were from the Philadelphia area. Girls on the "Nifties" were from Norristown and surrounding Montgomery County, and two came from Allentown. By the end of the season, a strong camaraderie was being felt from each team. If we didn't have enough players on one team, we would ask girls to change sides. But there was such a rivalry going on by that time, they didn't want to switch. So I was the utility player — I had two uniforms and I would play back and forth, play any position, and also got to play in every game!

The very last game we played that year was in Norristown. It was September, and I was four months pregnant. Before we left home, Harry said, "I don't think I'll play you tonight if we have enough players." I said, "Why not?" He said, "I don't want anything to happen to the baby and, if I know you, if you get in a bind and have to slide, you will." I said, "You are right." I sat on the bench until the ninth inning, when the first baseman jammed her thumb, so Harry put me on first base. The score was 5 to 4; the other team was winning. We were last at bat. The first girl struck out, the second girl got on first, the third girl grounded out to first base. I was fourth girl up, hit a solid hit about two feet above the second baseman's head. She missed it, and it was too low for the outfielder. I kept on running as I got to third base where a coach said, "Slide into home plate." As I did a hook slide into home plate, I saw Harry shaking his head as he came running to help me up. He said, "I thought I told you not to slide!" I said, "That was at home — I won the game, didn't I?"

I made Harry promise not to tell the girls on the team I was pregnant, because I didn't want a fuss made and, besides, this was between Harry and me. If Dad and Mom knew I was pregnant, I would have had to quit long before this. So this was "our secret" and, besides, I did not show any signs of being pregnant even though I was very thin. I gained only twelve pounds throughout my whole pregnancy. I was very fortunate to be in good health and still had no problem with my heart.

Harry was working at Frank Jones Sporting Goods Store in Norristown, and I had just quit my job at the hosiery mill in Lansdale. The stocking business was going down the drain due to the War; silk was too expensive, and exporting was too expensive, plus Japan was now "down and out" due to our Atom Bomb. Nylon thread was being experimented with, so a change in machinery and equipment was taking place. People were getting other jobs before they were told they would be laid off. The company did this by seniority. A couple of us girls in the sales department were there only a few years, so they started pushing us all around the mill to different departments. We didn't know from one day to the next where or what we would be doing. One day, my floor leader called me to her desk and asked me if I would go through the mill to all the Ladies Rooms and fill the Kotex machines. I said, "If I don't do it, what will happen?" She said, "Get someone else and you are out of a job." I said, "Okay, get someone else." I got my coat, left, and went home.

I was playing ball a couple of nights a week, and also Saturday and Sundays if games were scheduled, so quitting my job gave me more time to help schedule games and make phone calls to girls, letting them know what was happening in the coming weeks. I was out of work only a few weeks when Doc Dellicker was looking for a girl to take care of the soda fountain at his drugstore in North Wales and serve hot soup at lunch time. I asked him for an interview and he hired me on the spot. He knew Dad real well and also knew I could be trusted with handling money and making change. I caught on very quickly and just loved making sundaes, milkshakes, and jerking sodas. It wasn't long until I had most of the businessmen in town stopping in for hot soup and hot chocolate (which I had talked Doc into letting me serve). He told me he never had as busy a lunch trade until I came along. He said, "It's your pleasing personality, neatness, and good looks." He also gave me a raise.

I didn't tell him I was pregnant when I took the job because I figured he wouldn't have any trouble getting someone to replace me when I was ready to leave. This was the first job I truly liked since S.K.F. closed. I knew everyone in town and it was a joy to serve these townspeople; and I made friends with people passing through. It was the happiest six months on any job I ever had. I hated to, but told Doc I would work until Christmas, and then he would have to hire someone else. I trained a young woman whom Doc had hired by word-of-mouth. And one week before Christmas, 1950, I graciously bowed out — with many tears from customers.....and a $25.00 check from dear Doc for the new baby-to-be.

As I said earlier, I had a very good pregnancy, but I had a very hard delivery. Our precious baby girl was born Monday, February 19, 1951, at 7:30 p.m. in the Montgomery Hospital, Norristown. I was in labor 27 hours and, finally, the doctor had to use forceps to bring the baby along. I was knocked out so I knew nothing about the delivery. When I woke up, I saw a man holding my pulse and a nurse standing by his side. I was told later my heart had started to act up due to the long, hard delivery. To assist my family doctor, Emil Olson from North Wales, a heart doctor was called in by the name of Dr. Hudak, and also a baby specialist, Dr. Ruben.

I would like to tell you about the Friday night before I went to the hospital. Harry always worked until 9:00 p.m. on Friday nights, so it wasn't until around 10:00 p.m. he got home. I told him I was having terrific back pains and thought maybe the baby wouldn't be too long in coming. We went to bed and around 2:30 a.m. I was awakened with a funny feeling and had severe low pressure pains. As I got out of bed to go to the bathroom, my water broke. I called to Harry and he knocked on the bedroom wall to alert Mom, whose bedroom was next to ours in our rowhouse. She was by my side in a few minutes. As she was helping me back to the bedroom, Harry was lying on the bed stark naked, holding his head and saying, "Minnie, her water broke." She said, "I know, you crazy fool; put your pants on or get back into bed." He was so excited, he had forgotten to get dressed. (He never wore pajamas.)

93

Birthing a baby is quite common, but somehow men never seem to be able to handle it. This was just the beginning of a few quirks I was starting to find out about my new husband.

I was in the hospital ten days before I could go home. I had slight heart pains off and on for three days after delivery, and was so terribly tired. I had the baby on a Monday evening but did not see her until Tuesday evening. I was really a mess. When I was aware of having the baby and they told me it was a girl, I said, "I didn't want a girl; I don't know anything about girls." Doc Ruben said, "You're a girl." I said, "That's different; I wanted a boy. I have all brothers, so I thought I would have a boy. I don't know what I'll do with a girl." The Doc said, "We are going to bring her in to you. Now, if you don't want her, I'll take her along home. My wife and I don't have any children."

The head nurse was summoned to bring in the Stokes baby. When she put the baby into my arms, all I could see was her face which was all cut up — cuts between her nose, one eye all puffed up, and bruises at the temples. I started to cry and said, "What did you do to my baby? Where are her arms and legs?" The Doctor told the nurse to strip the baby so I could see the rest of her body. She was perfect, ten fingers and ten toes. The nurse dressed her again, wrapped her in a blanket and laid her in my arms. With tears in all our eyes, I finally knew I was a MOTHER. What a joy this little bundle would be to me and her Dad!

Harry only came to see me three times while I was in the hospital. I couldn't figure out why because he worked in Norristown only a few blocks from the hospital. Only years later did he tell me he thought I was going to die and he was scared to death of hospitals.

Two days before I went home from the hospital, the nurse said we had to name the baby. Well, we didn't have any girls' names picked out because, right from the beginning of my pregnancy, I thought I would have a boy. If so, it would have been Bradley Scott Stokes; instead, we named her Gail Jean Stokes. The "Gail" was from the "Gail Storm Show" that I used to watch on TV, and "Jean" was from Jean Pachella, my girlfriend, whom we were very fond of. Also Jean's husband, Eddie, grew up with Harry and we were together every weekend.

When Eddie found out Harry wasn't coming to see me more often, he pretended he was my husband and brought in a big doll for the baby (which Gail had for years).

Gail Jean and new momma were brought home to a house full of new baby toys, gifts, and most of all, a beautiful new decorated bassinet. We had so much company my first day and evening home from the hospital, Harry had to carry me up to bed, I was so exhausted. As I said before, we had lots of friends and also I was the last one in the family to be married, so all my brothers and sisters-in-law were really great supporters of Harry and me. My being the only girl in the Rogers family, my brothers were really catering to me, now that I was a little momma. I suppose for the first time in their lives I really proved to them I was a true girl, not just the little tomboy who tagged along after them.

Believe it or not, I took to being a new mother very quickly. I was very fussy about keeping the baby diapered and bottles sterilized. I was so sick after the delivery, the doctors decided not to have me breastfeed. This art of nature I never experienced, even ten years later when I had Scott.

Most of my friends were surprised to see the protectiveness and attentive care I gave to Gail. Being a tomboy all my life, they thought I would be haphazard or neglectful. Instead, I was a perfect mother. I think the reason for my strong parental attitude was due to the fact I thought I would never be a mother. I was so elated and thankful that I had this perfect baby, and also that I lived through this ordeal, and that maybe God had something in mind for me and my loving husband.

This was quite a new experience for Harry too; he was never around too many small children, except my nieces and nephews whom he grew to love. Being a new father put a feather in his hat, and he also did a lot of bragging. Such as "There was nothing to it" he would tell people.

Gail was a healthy, happy, and very good baby. When she woke up in the morning, I would bathe, diaper, and feed her, put her in the beautiful bassinet, and she would sleep for hours. I would sit and watch her sleep, and couldn't believe this beautiful baby was all mine. In fact, I really didn't want people to hold her or touch her too much, because I didn't want her to get any of their germs. What a protective mother I was.

I would like to inject at this time about the beautiful bassinet that was given to me to use until Gail outgrew it. We had friends by the name of Eleanor and Allen Swartz, who had a baby several months before I had Gail, but their baby died at birth. Eleanor's mother had decorated the interior of this bassinet with the most intricate detail that it was a sight to behold. Eleanor and her husband decided to share the use of it for our baby. What an unselfish thing to do. It wasn't too many months until Gail was outgrowing the bassinet that the Swartz's were expecting again, and this beautiful and meaningful bassinet would be put to use again. (Aren't friends wonderful.)

When Gail was six months old and growing very nicely, I would put her in a round washbasket and carry her all over the house with me. She was sitting up very well and was very alert. When I would scrub the floor, I would put her in the basket on the other side of the room and play peek-a-boo with her and make her laugh out loud. Mother came in one day and said, "Who were you talking to awhile ago? I thought you had company." I said, "Gail." Mom said, "If you keep that up, she'll be talking in no time."

I never talked "baby talk" to Gail; I always talked to her as an adult. I feel, as a result, she did talk very early. She was crawling all over and pulling herself up. She took her first step and, at eleven months, was walking and jabbering. What a joy!

Harry had an opportunity to take a salesman's job selling sporting goods equipment. Being a sales representative meant he would have to travel, and also give up his job at Frank Jones. It meant more money and also an advancement if he proved himself. Harry was quite an aggressive person, so we could see this job as opening up new horizons for him. This also meant I would be home alone all week with Gail until his return on Friday nights. I knew Harry well enough to stand behind him on this new experience, or have a dissatisfied human being on my hands. Also, we still had the girls baseball team to contend with and this job gave him Saturdays and Sundays free — which was when most of our games were scheduled.

Now, I might add, this girls baseball league was starting to invade our home privacy and was also taking expense money from our own pockets. We were just about breaking even, plus the fact over the winter months some of the girls got married, engaged, or lost interest, which meant we would have to start to look for new girls. We were beginning to realize it was eating into our personal lives now that we had a child and home to take care of. So we decided to make 1952 our last year but, as time marched on, the baseball team talked us into another year. So in the Fall of 1953, we decided to hang up our gloves and shoes — with a grand "Farewell Party" to all the wonderful lassies who shared a lot of good times and experiences none of us will ever forget.

About forty years later, when the movie A LEAGUE OF THEIR OWN came out, audiences took a renewed interest in these girl players. I found a photo of the "Nifties" but I guess I no longer have one of the "Fillies." As I think back on those good times, I wonder where they all are today. Some of our players on the "Nifties" were:

___?___ Braerby
Gail "Gussie" Brown
Betty Lou Cassey of Norristown
Verna Custer of Trooper
Joan Douglas
Angie Ermigiotti of Edge Hill
Shirley Estock of Center Square
Doris Heinsbach of Trooper
Betty Hoy of Norristown
Erma Keyes of Frazer
Gloria Manetti of Conshohocken
___?___ Miller
Dolores Osowski
Jeanette Penecale
Mary Jane Robbins of Norristown

Joan Scheetz of Norristown
Skip Scheid
Ruth (Rogers) Stokes of North Wales
Dolores Szulaski
Gert Woodland

I had kept my uniforms for years, sometimes using them as Halloween costumes. Then as they faded and got tattered and torn, I wore them to wash the car. Finally, they got thrown away — now how I wish I would have kept them. And when folks today ask me what kind of salary we girls received, they are surprised when I answer, "None — only our travel expenses were paid." We did it for the love of the game!

Harry was doing quite well with his selling job, but kept talking about starting a sporting goods store of his own. He knew he didn't have enough money, or where a good location might be, so this was just a lot of talk at the time.

Back in the Fall of 1951, Grandpaw Mock came to live with Dad and Mom. He was a joy. For the first time in my life I had a grandfather living close to me, whom I was just learning to know. He was a very gentle and loving man. Gail was just learning to walk and talk when he moved in with my parents, so she was quite a joy for him to play with. She would crawl over to him and pull herself up to him as he sat in his chair. He would look down at her and the next thing we knew she was on his lap. He would play patty-cake, and sing songs to her and make her laugh, as we were being entertained also. Gail was the fourth generation, so we had pictures taken of Gail along with Grandpaw, Mother, and myself.

As I said earlier, our grandparents had never lived near us, so it was a great satisfaction to spend time with him. My Dad's father had died when my oldest brother was a baby, and Grandma Rogers died when I was six years old. Since they lived in Western Pennsylvania, we didn't get to visit them very often. As a result, we never had a close relationship. That's why

I am posing with Gail at 18 months

Grandpaw Mock was such a joy to have around; however, this would end too soon.

In April 1952, Grandpaw Mock was getting out of bed, when he fell and broke his hip. He was taken to the hospital, but a few days later he developed pneumonia which made him quite weak. The doctors said there wasn't anything they could do, but let him rest. He was brought home from the hospital and Mom took care of him. He was getting weaker each day, even though Mother was giving him the best attention. I would go over in the mornings and help Mom bathe him and turn him so he wouldn't get bed sores. Mother was very fussy about the bed clothing. She washed his sheets every day and put clean bedding on every day.

Early on May 15, 1952, Mother knocked on my bedroom wall, calling me to come next door. As I started up her stairs, she greeted me and said Grandpaw had just died — she had been up with him all night. I said, "Why didn't you call me sooner?" She said, "I knew there was nothing anyone could do; his time was up." Mother was with her mother when she died; she was with her father when he died too. (Is this what family is all about?) Grandpaw Mock lived a good and long life; he was 86 years old and passed on a good heritage to the rest of us. What a gem!

This was the first time in my life I ever saw a death so close at hand, and I was realizing that "life is death, and death is life." As I said earlier, Grandpaw Mock was laid to rest in the Ogletown Church of the Brethren cemetery next to his first wife, and Grandmaw Mock was buried next to her first husband in Berkey Cemetery. Life is strange. Grandpaw Mock was the last of that generation, so now Dad and Mom became more precious to me, making me aware that life marches on and we should make the best of it.

Chapter 9

SPORTSMAN'S PARADISE

Dad and Mother had never taken a vacation in their lives. When they got an invitation to go to Florida from mother's sister and brother-in-law, they decided to go. Aunt Nellie and Uncle Jim Dailey had a mobile home in Jensen Beach, Florida, and had an extra bedroom. Dad and Mom left the second week in January, 1953.

It was the first time either one was ever South, so this was quite a pleasant experience for them. Mother said they had to take their heavy coats off in the Carolinas and didn't put them on again until weeks later when they were on their way back home. What a good time they had. Uncle Jim and Aunt Nellie were ardent fishermen, so they took Mom and Dad fishing quite often. Mom loved the ocean and beach, so she would wade the waves and look for all kinds of shells — and leave the fishing up to the rest of them.

It was the first time in our lives we saw Mom with a suntan. She looked great. They were gone six weeks and when they returned home, Gail ran out to meet them. When she saw Mother, she stopped, looked up to me and said, "Is that my Nannie?" We all laughed because Mom did look different sporting a Florida tan.

Dad and Mom had a great surprise in store for them when they came home — my brother Glen's wife, Esther, had given birth to a boy, Barry, on February 25, 1953. We were all delighted to have another baby in the family. He was a joy to all of us, but we were heartsick to learn later that he was a Down Syndrome baby and would not be like the rest of our children.

What a blow this was to Glen and Esther. They had waited ten years to have another baby. They had a healthy baby girl, then had the boy they wanted, only to find out he would not be normal. What a challenge life had in store for them. (I say, "Where is God; how could He let this thing happen to these two wonderful people?") Glen's life was saved from the War to come home to a loving wife and daughter and build a future together, only to have it torn to pieces with this new Down Syndrome baby. Could they handle this new challenge? Yes! And we as a family stood behind them. We loved Barry Glen just as we did the rest of the kids in the family. He brought lots of joy to all of us, and still does! (He is now 42 years old and lives in a group home in Harleysville.)

Harry was now doing quite a lot of traveling and was going to sports shows in Harrisburg and New York. He would have a booth and his job was to share with customers the new line of equipment for the coming year. He liked his job but was getting more restless. He really didn't like traveling all that much.

He started talking to me more and more about starting his own store. I said, "What are you waiting for? Why don't you start one?" He said, "It takes money and we don't have any." That sure was a good reason because he was just making enough to pay our bills then. I said, "Borrow the money." He said, "Who from; we don't own our own home so we can't borrow from the bank." I said, "I guess I'll have to go to work." He said, "Oh, no, Gail is too young to have a babysitter. I don't want anyone else raising our baby." I said, "Mother is just next door; if she will babysit, I won't have to take Gail out in all kinds of weather."

By then Gail was two years old. She was potty trained at eighteen months, and she was doing a lot of talking, so she really was out of the baby stage. When I approached Dad and Mom about my going to work, Mom said she wouldn't mind taking care of Gail, but Dad said, "A woman's place is in the home with her children." But then I explained that Harry would like to start a sporting goods store of his own, and we wouldn't be able to do it on one salary. Dad said, "Well, Mother and I can't help you financially but we can help with the baby and, of course, we don't want any money for doing it." (Aren't parents wonderful!)

The following week I started calling different employment offices and making personal contacts, but no one was hiring. I stopped at the drugstore I used to work in and, as I was having a Coke, I was talking to Ray Hartman, who worked for Doc Dellicker. He said he heard they were hiring girls at Lansdale Tube. The next morning I went over to Lansdale Tube.

I was fingerprinted and asked questions by the personnel man and filled out forms for a job. I didn't really care what I did as long as I got work. The gentleman who was fingerprinting me asked, "What did you do before you came here?" I said, "I was a housewife and mother, why?" He responded, "Because you have such strong hands." I laughed and said, "I was a ballplayer." He was interested and wanted to know all about the girls team. Well, this bit of news went through that whole office. I was hired and told to start work the following Monday.

My job was to put tubes onto an "ageing rack", which was an eight-foot-high machine with ten round discs across a board. It moved automatically and each disc had to have a tube put into it's socket. At the end of the process, each tube had the right amount of heat put through its housing. If there were any cracks or burnt out tubes, the girl on the other side of the ageing rack would sort them out and put them into the discard box.

As a result of the repetition, it became so automatic a procedure that I could do it with my eyes closed. I would sit and sing or whistle to pass the time away. One day I was singing real loud, doing my job, not paying attention to a pair of feet standing next to my machine. When I looked up and saw a very well-dressed, good-looking man watching me work, I gave him a big smile. He said, "Do you like what you're doing?" I said, "No, sir, any dummy could do this job." He said, "What would you like to do?" I said, "Something where you have to use your brains — the repetition of this job is for the birds." He laughed, walked away, and continued his observation of each machine, and greeted the foreman as he went from one aisle to the next until he disappeared into his office. The girl next to me said, "Do you know who that man was?" I said, "No." She said, "Mr. Steller, he's our Plant Manager!" Whether he was Plant Manager or President of the company, I would still have said the same thing. Every day when Mr. Steller walked through the plant, he always came over to say hello to me and make conversation.

The other girls got mad about that and a few let me know about it. This was a new experience, working in a plant with mostly women who were working just for an extra income, not wanting to better themselves, so their jobs were not important to them other than a job. Most of the women I worked with had started working in this plant during the War so they had quite a bit of seniority built up, plus Lansdale Tube had a profit-sharing plan so the future looked good to them. My being a new person with a personality and making friends with the plant manager rubbed these gals the wrong way.

Also it got known around the plant about my playing ball. I was approached about helping to start a girls softball team. Again, I was meeting heads of departments and was introduced to the people in charge of heading up a sports program. This was right up my alley, so I was slowly being drawn into the upper echelon of business heads. I told them I would help start a ball team but wouldn't have time to play.

Then one of the fellows asked me if I would like to start a golf group. Some of the women had been asked what sport they would be most interested in — golf came in as number one. So I said okay.

It just so happened the year after Gail was born, Harry had bought me a set of golf clubs. I dug holes in the back yard and put empty soup cans in them so I could learn to putt. I had never played before but Harry did, so he showed me how to hold the clubs. It wasn't long until my putting got excellent.

Then I would go up behind the high school to drive golf balls. When I thought I was good enough, I told Harry I was ready to play. He took me over to Norristown's Overbrook Country Club for my first game. He was quite impressed with me, so from that time on when I found time to play, I would go out on my own. I was soon beating him. He didn't have much free time to play so, as a result, I was getting better and he was mediocre.

Getting a golf group organized was a new challenge for me but a rewarding one. Lansdale Tube rented the Oak Terrace Country Club every Tuesday night so all we paid were the greens fees — this was feasible for all the girl golfers. Now again there were only a few girls who could golf, so the rest were learners. I divided the players into two groups, players and learners. The players were coupled off to play each other and learners were taught by the golf pro.

The golf pro at that time was a Mr. Kelly (I don't remember his first name). One evening he approached me and said, "How long have you been playing golf?" I said, "Just about a year." He said, "Who gave you lessons?" I said, "My husband when he had time." He said, "Would you consider letting me teach you?" I said, "I don't have the money or the time." He said, "It's too bad; you have the potential of a great golfer. I have been teaching quite a few ladies but have never seen one with such a strong swing." I told him I was an ex-ballplayer. He said, "That explains it; I wish you would reconsider my offer."

As Gail and I were going to the Ambler Church of the Brethren one Sunday in January, we rode past a new building at 318 Butler Pike with a "For Rent" sign in the window. When I got home, I told Harry about this new building that was for rent. I said, "Why don't we call Monday morning and ask how much a month the owner wants?" Harry said, "Where are we going to get the rent money?" I said, "I'm working, so let's find out how much they want and maybe we can start a sporting goods store." He said, "Ruth, we don't have any money to buy supplies, or money to advertise." I said, "How about word-of-mouth to our friends until it gets known. Also, I'll tell people at Lansdale Tube." He just shook his head and said, "You sure have guts."

That night neither one of us could sleep because now I had planted the idea in his head, and I knew for a long time he had the knowledge for selling and also had contacts with quite a few companies of sporting goods equipment. If he contacted them, they would probably put equipment in the store on consignment. Just before we fell asleep Harry said, "I have a $500 insurance policy; maybe I could cash that in."

The next morning after Harry went to work, I called the number written on the "For Rent" sign and talked to a gentleman by the name of Phil Sabella. I asked him how big the store was and how much rent he was asking. When Harry came home that night, I told him I had talked to the man who had the store for rent in Ambler and that he wanted $75 per month and would lease it for one year. Harry cashed in his insurance policy. The next day we signed a year's lease for our new store-to-be. Then

Sportsman's Paradise in Ambler—our sporting goods store for 23 years

in April 1954, we had an open house for the Sportsman's Paradise Store (a name I had suggested). Five hundred dollars and guts — we were on our way to a new, interesting future!

We decided at first just to be open on Friday nights and all day Saturdays until we could make enough money to pay someone to work during the day. We realized we both had to work at least six months until we could hold our own. I was now making almost as much money as Harry so I was contributing quite a bit to this new venture. Since I had more or less pushed Harry into this, I had to stand behind him.

He had quit his selling job at the end of January when he heard about an opening at a Tube mill where my brother Alvin worked. When Harry went for an interview, they hired him right away. In a few weeks' time, he was made Foreman of a night shift job that opened up. So that meant Harry could open the store from 9:30 a.m. to 4:00 p.m., sleep a few hours, and go on to the night shift job. He did this for five years — what a sacrifice just to have a business all our own.

I would like to inject at this time that I was quite well known by then at the Tube. I had worked there a little over a year and knew quite a few people. One day I was asked by Mr. Steller to come into his office. He said, "I have been watching you and notice you are quite popular with the workers and also understand you are on the sports program. Can you type?" I said, "No." He said, "I soon will be needing a new secretary and wondered if you would be interested." I said, "I can't type and also I don't think I could sit behind a desk all day and just type." He said, "Would you consider going to night school if we paid for it?" I said, "I'm sorry, I don't think I'm cut out to be a secretary, but if anything else would open up, I might be interested."

About a month later Mr. Steller called me into his office again, and he told me a new department was soon to be started in the lab and they were looking for new people to train for this delicate work, "Would you be interested?" I told him, "Yes, I will try."

Within a few weeks I was in a whole new environment of new faces, foreign-looking machinery and equipment. What a pleasant surprise when I found out I would be working with Doctors of Sciences, who had all kinds of degrees. What a change, and how lucky I was to be part of a new team of men working on special projects and some secret work for the government. The men I worked with were intelligent, aspiring young men with certain goals in their lives, and most of them were still going to night school to get their Doctorates in different sciences. We worked very closely together.

We girls who were selected to work with these projects were called Lab Technicians. Our job was to assist these men on their projects. They designed these very technical machines, with jet streams of water and chemicals surging through tiny plastic tubes into a silver germanium chip. The machines were programmed to stop at a certain depth on this chip, then the chip was put into another machine that dropped a certain amount of gold into the center, which acted as an adhesive for wires to adhere to for conductors; then later this unit would be encased in a tube-like shell. When the unit was finished, it wasn't more than a quarter-of-an-inch in size, so you can see the work was very delicate.

It was very fascinating and interesting work. I would get so involved with these men on their projects that, if a certain procedure didn't work according to theory, I would be just as disappointed as they were. We became very close as a working team. We were together eight hours a day and sometimes, if we were working on a project and had a deadline, we would all work overtime. So financially I was doing very well.

At this busy time of our marriage, we were seeing less and less of each other and it was starting to fray our relationship. I was so involved with this new job that I wasn't as concerned about the store, thinking anyway that it was Harry's new toy. And now I had something of my own that my abilities portrayed for me. Why not grasp it!

About that time, Dad and Mom moved back to Western Pennsylvania to take care of Aunt Sara Jane and Uncle Andy Rowser, who were up in years. Their daughter, Alice, had married a career Navy man, Joe Roberts, and she wanted to be with him. So she asked Dad and Mom to take care of her parents. Dad was now retired with not too much income, so this was an opportunity to go back to their roots. Since they didn't own their home, they could move without too much trouble — except from Mother.

That was the first time that I had ever heard Mom oppose Dad. She didn't want to leave us kids and, besides, this area had been their home for thirty-some years. All their friends were here. Remember earlier I told you how homesick Mother was when they moved down to the Montgomery County area years ago. But by now, she had learned to love the people, our church and, most of all, her neighbors. To leave those close relationships would again tear her apart. Mother had independence for the first time in her life. She would take the bus or train and go shopping or visit people. All that would be stopped if she were tied down to this elderly couple; she would really not have too much time of her own. But as usual, Dad won out. So the move was made, with many tears by neighbors and, most of all, by me

— Mom and I were very close. She was my best friend and, most of all, my loving Mother.

I had to get a babysitter for Gail, who was now three years old. We were fortunate to get a neighbor a couple of blocks away by the name of Blanche Hartman. Her husband, Ray, worked for Doc Dellicker for years, so we knew one another quite well and were thrilled when she said she would babysit Gail. In the meantime, I was working, taking care of the house, plus on Saturdays I went down to Ambler to the store.

At our rowhouse we had a bucket-a-day coal stove which had to be taken care of every day during the winter. Ashes had to be cleaned out every day, and the coal had to be banked every night and day to make sure it wouldn't go out. Well, most of the time when I got home, the fire was out and the whole house would be cold. Harry would forget to put coal into it or run out of time, so I was stuck with building new fires.

One evening I had just picked Gail up at the babysitter's after a trying day at work. When we went into the house, it was cold — the fire had gone out. I wrapped Gail in blankets and sat her on the davenport. I went down to the bucket-a-day stove and cleaned out the ashes. I was putting kindling wood in the stove, so I could put coal on top as the wood took afire, when Harry came running into the house to change clothes for his night job. I ran up the cellar steps — cold, mad, crying — and said, "If we don't get away from this nuisance, I'm going to burn the house down; then we'll HAVE to move!" Harry looked at me with his infectious smile, kept right on dressing, then walked over and gave me a peck on the cheek and said, "I'll see you tomorrow night."

That's the way our life was by that time. We didn't have time to talk to one another for a whole week. We would pass one another going and coming from work. He would be coming home from his night job and I would be going to work, so we would "toot" to one another. What a way to live! Would our marriage be strained by our lifestyle, which we had so innocently got involved in trying to make a decent living and build up our inventory at the store? I paid all the household and food bills with my money, and Harry was putting most of his into the store. Without realizing it, we were both becoming workaholics. We didn't have much time for entertaining and also could not be entertained because of our busy schedules.

Several nights later after the episode with the stove, I was reading the <u>North Penn Reporter</u> newspaper and saw an apartment for rent on the Taylor estate, located at Evans Road and Sumneytown Pike. I called about it and asked how much rent and how many rooms, then made an appointment to see it. It was the second floor of a carriage house, and it had two bedrooms, a nice living room and kitchen, with a lovely yard around back of the property. It would be an ideal place for Gail, and also it was in the country with very few homes close by. When I finally got to tell Harry about the apartment, my mind was made up to move. So he had to go along with me, or get someone ELSE to take care of that bucket-a-day stove!

When moving day came, our furniture was transported to the carriage house, but we had a problem with the davenport which I had just gotten reupholstered a few months before. It was about one foot longer than the stairwell entrance, no matter at what angle the fellows tried to steer it. Well, I guess you know my name was mud by this time. Harry said, "That's what you get when you watch those advertisements on TV." He was right. I had seen this ad on TV before Christmas — you get a davenport and one chair reupholstered for $150. They picked up and brought back new refinished furniture at no extra cost, but I didn't know they would change the style of the arms.

So now I had to go down to the big house on this estate and ask Mr. Keon whether we could knock out about a foot of his stairwell so we could get the davenport in. What a way to start off a new relationship with a property owner! But he was very gracious about it and said, "Just make sure the bannister is put into place and isn't weakened by its removal."

The Keons had come from Philadelphia and bought this estate from the Taylors. Later it was sold to the Catholic Diocese and is now the home of the Sisters of Mercy Academy.

We liked our new apartment and location very much but, to my dismay, these two apartments were heated by a large bucket-a-day stove! I found this out one evening when I came home from work with Gail. The apartment was cold, so I went to the

110

first floor apartment and knocked on the door. When it was opened, there stood a young woman with a bathrobe on and a large sweater over top. Her little boy was sitting on the floor with his coat on. I said, "Is something wrong with the furnace?" She said, "Yes, it's out." I said, "Who takes care of it?" She said, "My husband and I. It went out this afternoon and I didn't get to it on time so I thought the heck with it." (Well, I guess you know what went through my mind. Another darn bucket-a-day stove! Will I ever get away from them?) I was afraid Gail would catch cold so, being the old pro on bucket-a-day stoves as I was, I started the old stove and had heat up through the pipes in no time. That was my first mistake with this young woman, who was an in-law of the Keons.

I also soon found out she didn't like housework either. I went to work every day and spent most of Saturdays in the store, but my apartment was always neat and clean. She sat around all day reading, letting her apartment get cluttered and dirty. Lots of evenings I would hear her run the vacuum cleaner just before her husband got home, making believe she was cleaning all day. She would put her little boy, Guy, outside to play in the court-yard and, when Gail and I would come home, would ask me to keep an eye on him for her. (So she could sit on her derriere and read some more.) I always tried to spend time with Gail outside, before we went in for supper, so I was a sucker for this girl's request. Besides, I felt sorry for the little tyke, and it gave Gail a playmate.

The Keons were lovely people and were quite friendly with us. When Spring was just around the corner, Gail and I spent more time outside. I noticed there was an old chicken coop in back of the barn, near a few apple trees. I went down to the big house and asked the Keons if I could clean out the chicken coop and make a play house for Gail. They said I could. So the following night I stopped at the hardware store, got a gallon of white paint, went home, and started painting inside the coop. In a couple of days Gail and I had finished. We both had paint splatters on us, especially Gail who was 4 1/2 years old at the time — she thoroughly enjoyed being part of this new endeavor. I had some striped material left over from one of my sewing sprees, so I made a curtain for the only window in the coop. Gail had been given a table-and-chair set for Christmas, so we put that into the coop and brought her doll coach and a doll, plus some of her little books. I made a few shelves out of old wooden crates, so we could put her dishes and pots and pans on. It was quite a lovely play house by the time we were finished. Gail played many hours in it.

One evening while I was making supper, I heard Gail talking to someone. (I could look out the kitchen window and watch Gail playing in the play house and also see all of the backyard.) When I looked out the window, Mrs. Keon from the big house, was holding a little tea cup in her hand and Gail was making believe she was pouring her tea. Mrs. Keon was delighted with the play house and was quite surprised it had turned out as lovely as it did. She was quite a lady. When she would be working in her flower garden and Gail would see her, she would run down to Mrs. Keon and talk to her and would almost always come home with flowers in her hand for me. When I approached Mrs. Keon, wondering if Gail was getting in her way or maybe annoying her, she laughed and said it brought back memories of her daughter when she was a little girl.

I would like to share one more thing that happened at this wonderful country home. Gail was almost always a happy child and a joy to have around. But one Saturday morning I was cleaning the apartment. Harry had just left for the store, and Gail was playing in her bedroom. I don't know what made her cross, but she got her dander up about something or other. I didn't pay too much attention to her and finally I said, "Why don't you put your coat on and go outside and ride your bike around the courtyard?" She said, "No, I don't want to." I proceeded to get her coat and insisted she put it on. This made her really cross. Then she announced, "I'm going to RUN AWAY!" I said, "Just a minute, I'll get your suitcase." She watched me put some clothes into it, not believing what she was seeing. When I put her pajamas in, she knew I was cross too! I closed the suitcase, walked her to the door, put the suitcase in her hand, and said, "I'll see you." She went stomping down the staircase with the suitcase hitting every step, got on her bike, and rode around and around the circular driveway, contemplating what to do. All at once she stopped the bike, left the suitcase on the ground, came running up the steps, opened the door, and said, "Where will I sleep tonight?" I said, "I guess here, if you have no place else to go." (Aren't children joys!)

We have many fond memories of this home in the country, but we would soon have another decision to make.

Chapter 10

RUNNING A BUSINESS

Our store was holding its own, but Harry was getting annoyed at not having enough money to buy more stock. He could see by now that the business potential was there but didn't have enough capital to buy more stock and also didn't have enough invested so he could try to get a loan from the bank. As a result, he needed more money. My parents didn't have money and, when he approached his parents, his Mother said it was too big a gamble and also made the statement, "I don't think you know how to handle money." He was very hurt at the time for being refused. But many years later I found this statement true, to my dismay.

We had a friend who was still a bachelor, Gus Mazzanti, who had wanted to go into the business with Harry right from the beginning. I fought it, saying that if we couldn't do it on our own without a partner, then we should not try it. But as the months went by, we were still struggling. When Gus stopped by the house one evening, Harry was telling him how he would like to build up his stock faster but didn't have the money. Gus said, "Take me in as a partner and I'll borrow from my parents." I was against it right from the beginning, but Harry said that was the only way we would get ahead quicker.

Papers were drawn up by a lawyer, so in November 1956, Sportsman's Paradise had two owners. In the meantime, Gus had married his childhood sweetheart, Doris Bookheimer, who was also my girlfriend, and they moved in with her parents. Both of them were working, so they could save more money than we could. We had an apartment, a little girl whom I had to pay a sitter for, and also pay for half of everything at the store. It was really tight for us, but that was the price you paid when you engaged in this type of agreement.

I was still working at Lansdale Tube and really enjoying it. Harry was pushing me farther away from the store now that he had a partner, which was alright with me. It gave me more time with Gail, and also I could play golf every Saturday morning. I was getting more involved with my workers at the Tube, and only went to the store on Friday nights. Harry always insisted I come in Friday nights, which I continued all our business years. Also, I was bringing men from work to look over our golf equipment and, hopefully, to interest them in other merchandise. I might add that at that time we had no idea what our best-selling items would be, so we had a little of every sport represented. As time progressed though, fishing equipment became our Number One seller, with guns and ammunition second.

I believe that one of the reasons we had a harder time breaking into our business was we were not natives of Ambler. Neither one of us were descendants of any family from Ambler, so we were more or less "outsiders." Ambler had quite a large population of Italians, many of whom were descendants of expert stonemasons in great demand at the turn of the century to build the large mansions. They were brought to the area by Mr. Keasbey, who owned nearly all of Ambler. So we had to more or less prove ourselves to the community and I'll tell you one way this was done.

When Harry found out there was a three-acre lake on the Saint Mary's property, he approached the Mother Superior and asked if he could start a fishing club and also have winter ice skating on the lake. The lake could be managed by Club members, and half the proceeds would go to the Saint Mary's Orphanage. This was agreed upon and, for the first time, Ambler had a fishing club and ice skating which all members of the family could enjoy.

A club was formed called Gwynedd Valley Sportsman's Club. A few weeks before the regular season opened, the Club had "Fish and Pay" on weekends. The proceeds from this event gave the Club enough money to pay for fish to be stocked in the lake. The more members they got, the more stockings they could have. It was quite a success and, in time, had to have a closed membership of just so many because the lake wasn't large enough to handle the overflow.

The Club got permission from St. Mary's Orphanage to put outdoor lights around the lake. In the winter time, people came from far and near to ice skate. It was a very beautiful sight on a clear, crystal night to watch all the people skating and enjoying themselves. This Club served quite a few people over the years and it also helped bring in new customers. So again, Harry's insight for business was being shown.

I have to inject one episode from this time. Harry and one or two of the Club members would go to St. Mary's Lake and measure the thickness of the ice to see if it was thick enough to hold the hundreds of people they would get on Saturdays and Sundays. The men had decided that ice six-inches thick should suffice. Well, one Saturday morning Harry (and I think Tommy Koch) went to the lake to measure ice. Harry had on his Ten-X red hunting suit and hunting boots, he himself weighing about 210 pounds, plus twenty more pounds for clothing. He had started to walk on the lake with a measuring stick in his hand when the ice gave way. Harry fell through under the ice, touched the bottom, and came up through the same hole he had entered. The Good Lord apparently wasn't ready for him as yet, and saw fit for him to come up through the right place. When Tommy Koch brought him home to change his clothes, he shook his head and said, "It's just his luck to come up the same hole he went in; I thought he was a goner." Needless to say, when it came time to test the ice again, a rope was put around Harry!

Getting back to business partners and the future of the store, Harry and Gus decided to divide the first year's partnership profits by buying two new station wagons. Also, they decided they should each vote a different ticket — one to vote Democrat, the other Republican. Again, these decisions were made without my opinion or knowledge until after they were done, and then it was too late.

When it came time for hunting season or fishing season, Gus always took off the first day to go. He said, "I always did it before and I'm doing it now." This meant someone had to be in the store so, as a result, they decided to hire a man part-time who lived just across the street from the store. This nice old gentleman, Mr. Barry, was a retired bookkeeper from Keasbey & Mattison Company. He didn't know anything about sporting goods, but he was honest and could keep the books (which by this time was starting to become a problem). Neither Harry or Gus knew enough about keeping business records "according to Hoyle" — each fellow had been taking turns keeping the books, for a month at a time.

When I saw this was becoming a problem I said to Harry, "Why not let me go to business school a couple of nights a week to learn to type and learn bookkeeping because, sooner or later, I will probably be going into the store anyway." He said, "I don't want my wife to know my business." I looked at him and said, "Okay, handle it your own way, but don't ever say I didn't offer to help you." This remark put a strain on my relationship with Harry all the rest of our business years. Quite often I had to "bite my tongue" when there were times he needed my opinion or asked for my help, which was soon to happen.

Gus and Doris were married and both were working other jobs, the same as Harry and I. But Doris knew nothing about sporting goods and, as a result, she would never help in the store. But after she became pregnant with her first child, she would come down to the store with Gus just to have something to do. That way, she could see the operation of the store and get acquainted with the stock, and also learn to handle money and work the cash register.

Her hardest lesson, though, came when Gus couldn't make it to the store on time, so she decided to cover for him until he got there. A male customer came in and was looking at pistols. She showed them to him and he asked, "How much?" (Now what was happening lots of times, the fellows knew the prices or knew what catalog to look in for the prices so, as a result, they were not marked.) Doris, realizing this would be a good sale, quoted a price off the top of her head, but was way too low, and also gave the pistol to the fellow without his signing papers to buy firearms. Naturally the devious fellow took advantage of her. Harry and Gus sure did sweat that one out for several months. Needless to say, Doris wasn't asked to help very often.

Over the months Gus was beginning to get annoyed with Harry and his ways of doing things at the store — but being tied down to a business, working another job, and having a new-born baby and postpartum wife probably added to it. No two people do things the same way. Gus was meticulous; Harry was haphazard but energetic. Gus was impatient — he wanted to see results right away. Harry was imbued with long-term prospects of his strategy.

As a result, personality clashes were starting to brew. I received a call at work from Harry, asking me to leave my job and come down to the store right away. When I got there, Harry was on one side of the counter; Gus was on the other side. They were throwing the store keys back and forth to each other, and saying, "YOU keep the store; I don't want it!" Also watching this tossing act was a girl the fellows had hired a few months before, and she was throwing in her own remarks. First, I took her by the arm and ushered her out of the store telling her, "This is none of your business", and sent her home. Then I said, "Okay, fellas, what's this all about?" I listened to these two grown men babble on then said, "Let's close the shop, go home our separate ways, think about this thing, and make a decision tomorrow." (Remember earlier I said Harry didn't want me to know anything about his business but, when the chips were down, who did he turn to? ME! Thank God!)

We talked just about all night. I didn't go to work the next day. We didn't know what Gus would decide, but we both realized that we were putting more time, energy, and money into the business than Gus was. Harry had made up his mind that he wanted to keep this dream intact and maintain the partnership. But when we met again, Gus had decided he wanted to dissolve the partnership and would give us six months to buy him out. So we borrowed this money from the bank, and it took us five years to pay it back. We almost went under a couple of times because of this partnership dissolvement, but we managed to get through.

To this day I know Gus never realized the hardship Harry and I went through to pay back that loan. At that time he was mad and hurt, so it didn't matter to him. Our friendship could have been destroyed, but it wasn't. Nevertheless, some months went by before we were back to our good feelings about each other. Time IS a good healer. In 1958, the dissolvement of partnership was completed. I said, "Harry, don't you ever talk to me again about a partner. I will stand behind you once more; I'll be your partner; if we go under, we'll go together."

Chapter 11

TAKING TIME
FOR CHURCH

Having a business, a little girl, and both working other jobs, we were a very busy couple, but we found time to get more involved in church work.

After we got married and had Gail, I tried to take her to Sunday School as much as I could. I knew church was an integral part of family training. We all had it, and I know how much it hurt Dad and Mom when we were growing up during the Depression years when we didn't have a car or money to go to church. So here I was, a married woman and a young mother, trying to fulfill my Baptismal duties as a Christian and a member of the Church of the Brethren.

On one of those Sunday mornings, I was dressing Gail for church when she ran into our bedroom, jumped onto the bed to her sleeping Dad and said, "Daddy, why don't you go to Sunday School?" Hugging her gently he said, "Because I know it all." Then when Gail and I came home from church, Harry was reading some sports book. I was getting lunch ready and heard Gail say to her Daddy, "Mrs. Eisenhard, my Sunday School teacher says 'No one ever knows enough about the Bible'." The next Sunday when Gail and I were getting ready for church, Harry came out of the bedroom all dressed up and said that he was going along to church with us. We were a church family from that day on. (Out of the mouths of babes! Thank you, God, for little children.)

Harry was raised Presbyterian and attended church regularly when he was growing up, so he was churched. But I would have to say that the one thing that really kept Harry involved in our church was the ball team. The Ambler Church of the Brethren was recruiting fellows so they could be enrolled in the Church League in Ambler. When Harry was approached about playing, he soon found time in his busy schedule to participate.

In the meantime, we had just gotten a new minister by the name of Berkey Knavel. He came into our congregation at a time in the 1950s when a lot of changes were being made — not only in church policy, but nationally.

The TV was making us aware of happenings all over the world. Willie Mays, center fielder for the New York Giants, became "Rookie of the Year" as they won the Pennant in 1951, then in 1954 won the World Series. He was a black man making a name for himself and being respected by everyone for his talents as he skyrocketed to fame. TV quiz shows were becoming popular.

In 1954, physicist J. Robert Oppenheimer, who was in charge of developing the A-Bomb, was released from the Atomic Energy Commission because of his lack of enthusiasm to continue this nonsense. And Martin Luther King Jr., a black minister from Alabama, led his people to campaign for desegregated public transportation and to become registered voters — by his preaching of the gospel of equality and nonviolence, he gave the Civil Rights Movement a new nationwide impetus, but it cost him his life years later.

Marilyn Monroe became the new sex symbol due to her super-blonde hair, curvy body, and swinging bottom. Movies were at a high. And there were plenty of fads, such as Davy Crockett coonskin caps (which soared the price of coonskin pelts to $8 a pound), colored glasses worn to view a 3-D movie, twenty-two college boys cramming into a phone booth. High school kids started another fad by inventing Living Droodles which required a rubber face and a good punchline.

Bomb shelters were being designed for one's own backyard. Girls were getting poodle cuts; boys were ducktailing the back of their hair. People were leaving the cities, moving to the suburbs, looking for clean air, space, and green grass. This move brought more people into contact with one another, and suburban schools had to be enlarged. Recreation facilities were being sought after. Alcohol was being consumed by the truckload, and the sale of aspirin was in the millions of pounds.

Harry was now getting very much involved with our church. He, Gus Mazzanti, and Frank Brown were baptized on Friday night, December 17, 1955, at 8:00 p.m. by Berkey Knavel. What a baptism that was — all three men were big guys, so they wanted a private baptism. We wives of the three men were there, Helen and Stanley Davis were the Deacons assisting Rev. Knavel.

This rebaptism by trine immersion was very meaningful for Harry. Remember he had already been baptized Presbyterian when he was eighteen years old. His mother talked him into being baptized before he left for the Navy; I suppose the thought of his going into the service prompted Mrs. Stokes' decision. He didn't give it much thought at the time. He had gone to the Presbyterian Church ever since he was a young boy but he had never joined before.

Now being a grown man, Harry made the decision to be rebaptized into the Brethren Faith. I never pushed or nagged Harry to join our church. As I said before, it was Gail who started him going to church. He liked the warmth of the people, the simplicity of our services and what our church stood for; so this baptism was a new beginning for him. It was his decision to make a pact with God, to accept the Brethren Faith and stand up for what the church stood for.

As you may know, we Brethren do not believe in infant baptism (although we do have a baby dedication service). Baptism is undertaken only when you are old enough for accountability of your life. So this act of rebaptism Harry entered into was nothing he took lightly. He started studying the Bible and reading reference books. Also he was studying the different faiths — Catholicism, Judaism, Buddhism. His problem was he didn't have enough time to read the way he would have liked to.

He was now a Brethren and very much involved. He assisted me in teaching the Junior Class. Later on we were Youth Counselors, and then our greatest joy was teaching the young marrieds and singles — our class, called the Koinonias, was a challenge but very rewarding.

Harry was soon involved in District Programs which took him traveling great distances, and he wouldn't get home until way late at night. The more involved he got, the better he liked

Ambler Church of the Brethren, Ambler, PA

it. It was his nature to put everything he had into a project or whatever he was involved with.

As a young couple, we were caught up in this mass of confusion, trying to live a normal Christian life. Our church was also starting to grow. We were a church for people in transition, catching new people who had moved into our area to better themselves with new jobs as they still continued their schooling. So we were getting a good group of families with growing children and, as a result, we needed more trained Sunday School teachers.

A woman by the name of Helen Davis was in charge of the Children's Education Department at that time. She and the minister, Berkey Knavel, were working together, doing a superb job of getting the latest of teaching materials and updating teaching techniques to give a new trainee the best possible insight into this important position.

I was approached by Berkey and Helen about becoming a Sunday School Teacher. They needed a teacher in the Fall for the Juniors. I said, "I don't know the first thing about teach-

123

ing." They said, "Would you be willing to go to a workshop course at Juniata College in July?" Helen was going to take a refresher course given at Juniata by the General Brotherhood for new teachers and experienced teachers, upgrading the new Brethren material, and introducing new techniques of teaching.

Harry and I talked it over and decided I would take a week's vacation to do this if we could get a babysitter for Gail. As I said earlier, Dad and Mom had moved to Windber, PA. So when I called my parents and told them about this opportunity, and since it was to happen in July, they said to bring Gail up to them. As usual, Dad and Mom were very supportive.

Helen Davis and I went to Juniata College the week of July 28, 1957. It was one of the most inspiring and rewarding endeavors I had ever encountered at that time of my young spiritual life. I was thrown in with very educated and dedicated women from all over the United States. This was a tremendous awakening for me. I was always aware of the pastors being rather well-educated, but didn't realize how many women in the Church of the Brethren held such high positions, plus the fact they were now being recognized as excellent leaders and had a lot to offer. I was impressed with their knowledge and, most of all, their dedication to teach new methods so that we as lay teachers could go back to our home churches and share this wealth of knowledge with our children. We were made aware of filmstrips, books, arts and crafts, and resource people who could be obtained through the Brotherhood. It was quite a boost for a person involved with teaching to have all these supportive things for helps. So I had a week full of training, which I used the rest of my teaching career and thoroughly enjoyed.

As time marched on, I was still working at Lansdale Tube, and Harry was still working the 3:00-11:00 p.m. night shift at Precision Tube. He was made a Foreman, given raises, and given the opportunity to work overtime, which he refused because he still wanted to run the store.

I would go to the store in the evenings from 6:00-9:00 p.m., after working eight hours at the Tube. Customers asked for Harry by his given name, but they had a special nickname for me — "Mrs. Sport." (I liked that.) And we had hired a gentleman part-time by the name of Ernie Spurlin and he was a terrific help to us. He knew sporting goods because he had been a sales representative. He worked for us until Harry decided to quit his nighttime job. The business was doing well enough for Harry to make a living as long as I still held my job. And then we had an opportunity to buy a home in Ambler. (It's interesting how things happen in life and, again, I know God had a hand in it.)

We were approached by Charles Haff one Sunday morning after church. He was a Deacon and a retired engineer from Keasbey & Mattison Company. He said, "The Mrs. and I are going to move down South. We would like to sell our home; would you be interested in buying it?" Harry and I looked at one another and said, "We don't have any money to buy a home." He said, "Think about it; maybe we can work something out." On the way home from church I said, "Boy, do they have a lovely home; I've been in it with my parents. It's neat and clean and has the most beautiful hardwood floors." Harry said, "Ruth forget it; we couldn't handle a mortgage right now."

It just happened that Dad and Mom called us that night. I told them about the Haffs' approaching us that morning about their home. Dad said, "It is a very well-built home and, of course, you would be near your business and the church. Did he quote a price?" We said, "We didn't ask because we knew we didn't have any money for a down payment." Dad said, "Just be patient and maybe things will work out!"

With that in mind, we tried to save as much money as we could, without putting it all into the store. About six months later, Mr. Haff stopped in the store and said he and Mrs. Haff had bought a home in North Carolina. Would we now like to talk about buying their home? He quoted a price to us and said that he would hold a second mortgage for us if we could get enough for the down payment. They wanted to move the first week in July, 1957.

We sure did a lot of scrounging around to get enough money for the down payment. Within a few weeks, we had negotiated with a real estate company and two days before the settlement, Mr. Ahler called us. He said everything was set for Wednesday; for us to bring our check and also a settlement fee of $900. Harry came home from the store that night and said, "Ruth, we need $900 more for the settlement fee. We don't have it; I guess we'll have to call it off." With tears in our eyes, we looked at each other, perplexed, not knowing what to do.

Just then the phone rang and it was Al Dummeldinger from church, who wanted to talk to Harry about the Church ball team. Harry told him about our not having enough money for the settlement fee, and that we couldn't borrow any more from the bank at that time due to our business loan. He said he guessed we would have to drop the whole thing. Al asked, "How much do you need?" Harry told him and he said, "Don't worry; I'll drop it off to you tomorrow at your store." Harry said, "But we don't know when we can pay you back." Al said, "Whenever you can."

You never saw two more excited people as we both were at that time! That night when we went to bed, we thanked God for people like Al and Betty Dummeldinger and Mr. and Mrs. Haff who had enough faith in us to help us buy our first house. We were ever so grateful, but now we had our store obligations plus an added responsibility of mortgage payments. Time would tell whether we could handle it or not.

As I said earlier, Berkey Knavel was our pastor at that time. When Helen Davis and I met at the church Saturday morning, prior to leaving for Juniata College, Berkey was there to wish us well and he said a prayer for our guidance for the week.

The next day being Sunday, all us ladies at the workshop were coming out of the Stone Church of the Brethren, Huntingdon, Pennsylvania, after the service, when Helen was summoned to the phone. When she came back to me, she had a strange look on her face. I said, "What's wrong?" She said, "Berkey just resigned from our church — he announced it from the pulpit this morning!" We were both so shocked and hurt we didn't talk all through lunch, each thinking her own thoughts. Mine running such as, "Why did he ask me to be a teacher in the Fall when he wouldn't be there to care?" He was an important part of our life. He baptized Harry and counseled with him when he was making the decision to join our church. He was very dynamic in the pulpit. He was building up our church membership. Why? Why? What were we as a church not giving him to keep him satisfied? Was it monetary, prestige, or what?

I remember sharing these things with Dad, and he said, "One of the biggest mistakes a congregation can make is to think a particular pastor can never be replaced, but they can. If you are going to be a strong church, you will all work together, pray together, and sooner or later everything will fall into place. Also remember, pastors have a right to choose what they want too. So it's best not to get all wrapped up in one individual, but do your own thinking, reading, and soul-searching. Pastors move on, but you may be in the same location much longer so, therefore, a church should stick together. Remember, a congregation can make or break a church."

With these words of wisdom, Harry and I kept on working for the church. Soon we were the first husband-and-wife teaching team that the Ambler Church of the Brethren ever had. I also sang in the Church Choir and was put on the Christian Education Committee. So we were really involved. We were both growing spiritually and enjoying it.

We moved into our new home at 909 Butler Pike, Ambler, in July, 1957. In fact, Harry and the men from the church moved our furniture from the Keon's carriage house to our home the Saturday Helen Davis and I came home from our week at Juniata College.

What a week! Our minister, Berkey Knavel, had resigned from the pulpit a week before, and six days later we were moved into our new home. It was a lovely, well-kept house. I didn't have any cleaning to do to prepare the home because Mrs. Haff had it all scrubbed for me, knowing I had been away all week. What beautiful people they were!

Moving from an apartment to a house is a big jump for a child. I did not realize this at first, but Gail would follow me all over the house — if I got out of her sight, she would call out and ask where I was. She now had a nice, big bedroom which we had fun decorating. We all enjoyed our new home very much. It was easy to clean. We had beautiful hardwood floors and a lovely big kitchen. We could do a lot of entertaining.

But we were only in our new home a few months when Gail came down with rheumatic fever. We had to put her in the hospital for a few weeks. We didn't know just how serious it was, so we were quite upset. Also, I knew I couldn't take off work too long. Again our faith was being tested. How could we afford a hospital bill with no insurance or hospitalization? How long would Gail have to lie in bed when she came home from the hospital?

Gail had been in school only a couple of weeks when this happened to her. If she missed too much school, she would have to be tutored. We called Mom and Dad in Windber. As usual, dear Mom came by Greyhound Bus to Philadelphia, and Harry picked her up. She stayed with us for a month as Gail got stronger each day. (God bless mothers, especially mine.)

Gail was allowed to go to school a few hours each day and then had to come home to bed the rest of the day. This went on for a month as she was progressing to normal strength. Thank God her heart was not damaged. She healed quickly and soon went to school all day, but she went to bed early every night. The next few weeks she had back homework to do to catch up with her class. By the Christmas Holidays she was all caught up, and by New Year's was up with her class.

As I said, Mother stayed a month with us. While she was with us, she said how much she disliked having to go back to Windber. She missed all us kids. We all lived within a few miles of one another, and they came to visit her often while she was caring for Gail in our home. One evening when I came home from work, she said, "Isn't this house too big for you to take care of with your work and having to help in the store?" But I didn't think too much about it at the time.

A few months after Mother went home, we received a phone call from her and Dad with the news that Alice and Joe Roberts were coming home. Joe was retiring from the Navy and now they would be coming home to move in with their parents. This meant Dad and Mom would not have to stay any longer to look after Aunt Sarah and Uncle Andy. That was the reason that they moved to Windber; now they were no longer obligated to that charge. I shared Mother's feelings with Harry and he said, "Where are they going to go?" I said, "I don't think they decided as yet; wouldn't it be neat if they moved in with us?" Harry said, "Give them a call and tell them we have plenty of room."

Dad and Mom moved in with us December, 1957. What a Christmas that was! Our whole family was together again. Now our home was always busy with nieces, nephews, brothers, and sisters-in-law. Whenever there were picnics or parties, they always wound up at our place. Now we had three generations in one home. What a joy! Mother and I got along very well, as we always did. We worked side by side in the kitchen, and never a cross word was spoken by either one of us.

Mother was always busy making pies, cooking, and just being her pleasant self. What a help for me. She had all our meals ready for us when we came home from work. She also cleaned the house and did all our washing and ironing. Boy, was I being spoiled! Harry took advantage of this and gave me more jobs at the store — picking up and delivering worms, and running to Philadelphia or Harrisburg for hunting and fishing licenses. We were really getting busy at the store.

Dad turned our garage into a carpenter shop and was getting odd jobs from the neighbors, plus was making shelves and fixtures for the store. Harry always had some new project going which needed carpentering, so this kept Dad busy and happy at the same time.

Again Dad and Mom got involved with the church which they had grown to love before their move. Mother would go to quilting every week because she could walk to the church. When a funeral dinner was held at the church, she was always one of the first women called to help. What a joy for them in their golden years to be involved again with this church, and also seeing their children every week. It was like old times with the kids coming home every Sunday and having a family fellowship once again. Remember, we were a close family. Dad and Mom continued living with us until they died.

Harry and I were still teaching Sunday School and were very involved with the church and its activities. After Rev. Berkey Knavel left our church in 1957, we had supply ministers until August, 1958. At that time Rev. Donald Kline arrived to fill our pulpit.

Harry was called upon quite a bit at that time to assist in the church programs on Sunday mornings. He would never say "no", no matter how busy he was otherwise, or how late he would have to stay up and study to prepare for those chores. He was constantly pushing himself, as if he had so much to do and so little time to do it — and that was true of him until his death.

We became quite close to Don and his wife Inky. They were the same age we were and, having no children of their own, Inky took a liking to Gail. Inky was an accomplished pianist. As a result, Gail got interested in the piano. We didn't have a piano, but soon the idea was planted into our heads by Inky that Gail was old enough to learn to play. Needless to say, on Christmas 1958, Gail got a piano. (In the meantime, she was taking lessons from Inky and would come home from the minister's house to practice playing her fingerings on the windowsill.) When the Klines left in 1960, Gail was very sad to lose her piano teacher and good friend.

Several months went by when I made a remark to a neighbor lady, Ethel Fillman, that Gail's piano teacher moved away and that I didn't know anyone else who taught piano. She gave me the name of a maiden woman in her church who taught piano. I started Gail with this piano teacher, but it was a disaster. After a few weeks of lessons with her, Gail would get pains in her stomach and just about throw up when I would get ready to take her for her lesson. Finally, I said, "Gail, what is wrong? Why do you act this way when it's time for your piano lesson?" She started to cry and said, "The teacher hollers at me and scolds me if I don't play right." I looked into this matter and found out this maiden woman was a perfectionist with her music, plus the fact that she didn't seem to know how to relate to children. As a result, Gail's piano days ended. She never took lessons since then, but still has her piano.

In 1960, we got a new minister by the name of Rev. Donald Rummel, who came to our church at a time when quite a few young people were having babies, so lots of things were happening at that time. Our church leaders at Elgin, Illinois, were sending out new methods for the churches to try, such as reorganizing the church body into Boards to get more people involved in the mechanics of the overall church program. We became involved with Don and his wife Helen very quickly, and with their two little girls. Echo was the older girl and she had red hair and freckles. The younger one, Lynette, had light brown hair and was very thin.

I was awakened one Saturday morning by an awful, shrill hollering and screaming. I jumped out of bed and went into the next room where this terrible noise came from, and there were these two little girls in a squabble over a hairbrush. It seems their Dad and Mom had to be at a District Meeting early Saturday morning and had asked Mother to babysit. But instead of going to their house, Mother had asked them to bring the girls over for the night, so she could also be with Gail while we worked all day on Saturdays. This was the beginning of a good relationship with this family.

Our business was starting to thrive. Harry had quit his night job at Precision Tube and was putting all his time into the store. As I said, he was involved with the Gwynedd Valley Sportsman's Club which he started, plus involvement at the church, plus community projects. We still didn't have a lot of time together as a family. I was still working at Lansdale Tube every day, so Saturday was my day to spend with Gail. We no longer needed a babysitter for Gail since Dad and Mom had moved in with us. If I didn't have to do any running for the store, Saturday was "our special day" to shop, go to lunch, or just take a ride out into the country and eat a sandwich under a tree. Mother loved to go out to the little creek that ran along our old homestead in Mainland.

But this sometimes became a strain on him and on our homelife – we as a family needed him too! As a result, our marriage was weakening. I was very happy for him but I also would have liked to have more time with him. Even Gail would say at times, "I didn't see Daddy for a couple of days; he must be busy." Harry would be up and out of the house before she came down for breakfast and wouldn't come home until she was in bed at night. However, he always went into her bedroom and kissed her. (She was the apple of his eye!) He would bring her gifts and toys to try to make up for not giving her more time. His assumption was that Mother, Dad, and I were always there for her, so this let him "off the hook."

I shall never forget the time he was playing Santa Claus at our Church Christmas Party. Gail was about five or six years old. He made the grand entrance with his Santa's outfit, and with a large bag of toys slung over his back. He started handing out the toys to the children and, of course, Gail was the last one to receive her gift. As he handed it to her she said, "Thanks

Daddy!" The whole room burst into laughter. Later that night he said, "I can't even fool my own daughter; I thought since she hadn't seen me much lately, she wouldn't recognize me." We both laughed and I said, "Gosh, you had ME fooled."

Chapter 12

MARITAL STRIFE

One day the big boss called me into his office and said he was hearing good reports from my co-workers — that I was very alert, caught on quickly, and took orders quite well. He said, "How would you like to go to night school at Drexel to learn about electronics, and take some chemistry subjects?" I was quite flabbergasted, but elated about this opportunity. He said, "Think about it for a couple of weeks; all your expenses will be paid for by the Company, but you will have to sign an agreement to work for us. We need some alert women who are intelligent, and besides it looks good for the Company to have women in its midst."

Here I was twenty-nine years old, married, a working mother, with a new business I was sharing with my husband, and now I had an opportunity to go to college. Decisions! Decisions! When I shared this news with Harry, he said, "When are you going to find the time to help me, and also what about Gail?"

I thought about this opportunity the Company was giving me. I wasn't real happy with our marriage then because Harry didn't make time for Gail and me the way he should have. He would always give everyone else the extra time he had, but pushed us off, and we were supposed to understand. It was almost to the point we weren't even sharing much of a conversation unless it was about the store or church work. He didn't share too much of the business end of the store with me. He had hired a young fellow by the name of Norman Hamilton, and he was a terrific help. Norman was a bachelor so his time was his own — working evenings was no problem for him. So that gave Harry more evenings to do his extra projects, again taking him away from us.

My biggest hurt with Harry at that time was he would promise Gail he would do something with her but, when the time came, she would be waiting and he would not show up. He forgot because he was too busy doing something else. This started pent-up feelings with me. When the boss at Lansdale Tube gave me this opportunity, it was hard to decide. (I thought to myself: "I could be independent, and maybe I don't need a man. I'll get this degree and when I am finished my courses, I can step into a good-paying job.") I started to pray about this. I was hurt with Harry. My love for him was slowly dying. (I thought.) I did a lot of soul-searching. Mother knew there was something wrong, but she never said anything.

One day I told her about this offer at work and said I wasn't sure what I should do. She said, "If you take that offer, you will be pushing yourself farther away from Harry. He needs you but doesn't know it just yet." (Mothers are so understanding and so supportive in their own subtle ways.) My faith too was slowing ebbing away, or so I thought, because God didn't seem to be answering my prayers.

Harry came in from the store a few weeks later and said, "Ruth, I need you at the store; we are getting so busy. I can't see hiring someone else when I can use you." I asked, "What about my job? Can you handle the bills here at home plus the store?" He said, "Yes, I think we can."

Now I had a decision to make. Spring was coming, which was a busy time at the store. If we didn't make enough money to pay our house bills after I quit work, then what? (Decisions, decisions; prayers and more prayers. Okay, God, I'll put my life in your hands.) I thought if I'm to be a good wife and mother, I'll stand beside my husband. After all, I'm the one who talked him into this business venture.

I went into work the next day and told my boss I was going to quit my job, saying, "My husband needs me more than your Company does." He was shocked, but he knew I had made up my mind and he couldn't change it. I worked until the first of July, 1960.

What a farewell dinner our gang at work had for me! I had never had any trouble with these co-workers. We had a terrific camaraderie relationship, and the engineers I worked with were super guys. Unbeknownst to me, they set up an airplane ride for me from the Lansdale Airport 202 to the Allentown Airport. (I had made the mistake of mentioning one day on our lunch period that I would never want to go up in an airplane; I wanted both of my feet on the ground.)

Well, two of my co-workers were pilots and they set this joy ride up for me as a going-away present. Everyone was in on this surprise, from the big boss on down. I was told we were going to Allentown for lunch. I said, "How can we get to Allentown and back within an hour?" They said, "Never mind, we'll show you." As we were riding toward the airport, I said, "This isn't the way to Allentown." They answered, "It is for us."

As we pulled into the 202 Airport, I saw a Piper Cub warming up and, as I was helped out of the car, one of the fellows said, "Here we are — we're taking you to Allentown for lunch!" I took one look at the small plane and started to run towards the car. They both grabbed me while kicking and put me into the plane. I hollered, "Did you tell my husband you were going to do this?.....I have a little girl I love very much!.....Do you know I don't have any life insurance?" I was thinking of everything I could to stop them, but they were strapping me in. I added, "I know I'll get sick!" I was handed a plastic bag.

The takeoff was smooth, but I wouldn't open my eyes. My stomach was churning. They told me to look out and take deep breaths — it was quite interesting how the countryside looked from that height. As we were landing at Allentown, my stomach was doing flip-flops, but they insisted on taking me into the restaurant for lunch. I said, "I can't eat; if I do, I'll upchuck all the way home." (We ate.) On our way back, just as we were going over Hatfield, I announced, "I'm going to be sick!" They said, "Use the plastic bag." I puked from Hatfield to Lansdale. Until we landed and I had both feet on the ground, I didn't think I'd ever be a whole person again. All the people of my working crew were waiting for us at the gate, cheering and laughing at this brave soul who was "green at the gills."

I shall never forget those co-workers and bosses as long as I live. It was a terrific experience and a growing time in my life, but now I was going to leave this in the past and start a new future alongside my husband.

God sure does work in mysterious ways. My days afterwards involved Sportsman's Paradise — we were enlarging the store, knocking out walls and changing merchandise from one part of the store to another, trying to make room for new equipment. Harry always had new ideas floating around in his head and, as a result, we were always busy with one thing or another. Lots of times I would have to drive to New York or New Jersey to pick up merchandise and do a lot of running so Harry could spend more time in the store — everyone wanted to talk to the boss, so it was necessary for him to be there.

Chapter 13

OUR LITTLE BOY

In September, 1960, Gail had to have a doctor's check-up for school and, as Dr. Kip was examining her, she looked up at him and said, "Can you do something to Mommy so she can have a baby?" He looked at me, laughed, and said, "Yes, I think I could but I don't think your Daddy would like it. Would you like to have a little brother or sister?" She said, "I'd like to have a little brother."

Harry and I never talked too much about having more children. We were both happy. Gail was a normal little girl. Also, I knew Harry was scared to death when he thought I was going to die when I had delivered Gail. And, we were very busy with our lives; we didn't have time for more children, especially Harry. And again, I would have been the one to stay home with a baby, so I never thought much about it, although I knew Gail was lonely at times. She would come home from school and tell about a classmate's mother having a new baby. Sometimes she would ask me why she didn't have any sisters or brothers. I would put her off by saying she was so precious to us we didn't need any more.

During the Fall of 1960, we were busy with hunting season coming along. We were selling guns and hunting equipment. But the most time-consuming task was filling out the hunting license forms. We only got a dime for each license and, with all the bookkeeping that went into it, it wasn't worth it. But hopefully, through this service, the customer would buy more items of value.

We were now meeting new people all the time at the store. Word-of-mouth from one satisfied customer to another brought in more business. Harry always made it a rule to know each and every piece of merchandise, so he could talk intelligently about it. Also, myself and the fellows who worked for us were given magazines and articles to read. So we had a good reputation as salespeople.

Harry had the opportunity to go hunting the first week in October with a customer by the name of Ed Simmers. He had a farm in Dushore, Pennsylvania. Knowing Norm and I could handle the store while he was gone, off he went. I felt that when Harry had these opportunities, he should go — I knew he needed to get away from the store once in a while. A hunting trip would also give him a chance to use certain guns, ammo, and equipment for a stronger sales pitch. In our business we were always planning ahead, so when Harry could say, "I used such-and-such a gun with this ammo and got good results", the customer always benefitted from his knowledge.

Working together at the store, Harry and I were together quite a bit now, and our time was very precious to both of us. We grew closer and finally I was being confided in about the business, although he still didn't want me to know certain aspects of the business and didn't let me handle the money. However, I should have insisted because I could handle money better than he could (which the future would unfold).

As a result of Harry's week away, he came home rested, I became pregnant, and by Christmas we shared our joy with the whole family. We were both so happy. Especially me — I was on cloud nine.

By the way, here's how we told Gail about our having a baby. After we opened all our Christmas gifts, Harry handed me this big, beautifully wrapped box. When I took out the contents, there were two beautiful maternity dresses. Gail looked at Harry and then at me and said, "Those dresses are too big for you, Mommy." Harry said, "But they won't be in a couple of months." Gail's mouth opened wide and said, "Are they maternity dresses? Are we going to have a baby?" Gail was so excited she said, "I'm praying for a little brother!"

I told Harry, "Let's keep it quiet for awhile to everyone else, because they'll find out soon enough." But he was so elated about being a father again, he couldn't keep it to himself. Our pastor, Don Rummel, was the first person Harry told, other than family members. It was to be their secret, but Harry couldn't keep it a secret for very long. I think the whole world knew about our new baby coming long before I went into maternity outfits.

Mom, Dad, Harry, Gail and I had tears of joy for this new event that was to happen in the near future. What a Christmas that was. We as a family always had Christmas dinner with the Stokes family. That year Harry's brother and sister-in-law, George and Peggy, had dinner at their home. We were all seated around the table and Peggy was serving the last dish of goodies from the kitchen, getting ready to sit down, when she said, "Does anyone have anything they would like to share with us?" Gail piped up and said, "My mommy's going to have a baby!" Peggy almost dropped the dish she was holding. Again more tears of joy!

We had a very good Christmas at the store that year and I was putting in a lot of hours. I picked up a cold and couldn't seem to get rid of it. By the end of January the Doctor told me if I didn't get this cold under control, I might lose the baby. He said, "Why don't you go to Florida for a month or two?" When I told Harry, he said, "Why don't you and John go? Minnie can take care of Gail and me." I said, "Where will we get the money?" He said, "Don't worry about that." Dad and I packed and, in a couple of days, we were on our way to Florida. We had relatives in Jensen Beach, Florida — James and Nellie Dailey (Mom's sister and brother-in-law) — so we had a place to stay. When they found out I was going to have a baby, they said, "Stay with us as long as you like."

That trip was the first time I was ever alone with my Dad for such a long time. I was going to be 36 years old in September 1961, and I was just now getting close to my father. Mom and I were always very close, but Dad always seemed to be strict and a little straight-laced, but fun at times. Life always seemed more serious with him. Driving for hours alongside of someone, either you do a lot of talking or you keep quiet and look out the window. Well, we talked and talked.

I shared my feelings with him — such as my life with Harry, the store, the church, what I wanted for Gail, and now this new baby. Dad said, "You have a lot of responsibility being a parent. It takes two to share your ideas and be firm with your discipline. If you stick together on this, you shouldn't have too many problems. Make a strong home life for your children, church them, love them, and set good examples. That's all anyone can hope for out of life. When some children reach a certain age, they never want to listen to their parents, but as they reach adulthood, most of their home training will come into being."

We had a wonderful time in Florida; the weather co-operated and the sun was doing me a world of good. In two weeks my cold was drying up. Aunt Nellie would put a lounge chair out front for me and every day I soaked up the sunshine. We would go out to the beach and fish if it wasn't too windy. I had more fun with Uncle Jim than I had ever had before — he was always aloof and stern to me as a teenager — but now he was warm and fun to be around. Maybe being around a woman who is pregnant brings the best out of men. Anyway, he would cast the ten-foot fishing pole for me and then hand it to me to pull in the fish. Dad got a big kick out of my standing in the ocean reeling in the fish.

We stayed with them two weeks and then went to Ann Marie Island to Harry's Uncle Burt and Aunt Kay Stokes. They had moved to Florida a couple of years before our trip and were always after Harry and me to come see them, but we had never had the time or money. Now Dad and I were on our way to Florida's western coast to see these two lovely people whom Harry and I liked very much. They made us quite welcome and were happy for Harry and me because of the event that was to happen at the end of July.

Uncle Burt made arrangements to take Dad and me out on a fishing boat a few days after we were at their home. What a fun day for me! I caught the biggest catch of the day and won the "fishing pool" with a 30-pound grouper. When the fish had grabbed my line, I thought I had someone's line, because the boat was crowded. Then as I reeled the line in, I could feel the fish tug. I hollered, "Uncle Burt, help me!" He said, "You bring it alongside the boat; I'll net it." My tummy was just starting to protrude, so I laid it on the rail of the boat and kept reeling!

We took pictures and Uncle Burt had it put in the paper. We had something special to write home about. It was February 14, 1961, and I called home to Gail. When Gail heard my voice, she started to cry and asked me when I was coming home and "...please don't have the baby down there." I told her we had several months to wait. She cried and cried, and soon I was in tears too. Dad talked to Mom and, at the end of the conversation, I heard him say, "I think we'll soon be home." Two days later we were packed and on our way to Pennsylvania. My cold was gone and I was ready to go home. We got home for Gail's tenth birthday on February 19th. Although my cold was gone, I did get tired quickly. The doctor didn't want me to work too many hours.

Back at the store, we were going into the Spring season and our fishing trade was picking up tremendously. Also Harry had bid for some of the baseball team business in the area, which he got. This meant he had to go out at night and measure the guys for their uniforms. If Norm got too busy, I would have to go to the store at night. Dad and Mom weren't happy about this, but it had to be done. Dad didn't know enough about sporting goods to help, so he felt helpless not being able to give some of his time. He would come down and pick me up at night so I would not have to walk home — we only had one car, so this was Dad's way of helping.

Harry joined a "buying co-op" with two men from Reading, PA. The one gentleman, William DiSalvo, had worms flown in from Canada. He had them picked up at the airport and stored them in his father's bar room cellar — which had a large walk-in refrigerator. If Harry was too busy to pick up worms, I would. Sometimes I'd take a girlfriend along to shorten the time, because it was an hour-and-a-half each way. So the trip didn't seem long with company.

When I would get back to the store, the worms would have to be packed into cartons. This was a job we were all supposed to do, but I was the one usually stuck with the majority of the packing — the fellows always seemed to find something more important to do. Sometimes we would let Gail help after school. She got a big kick out of it and, of course, her Dad paid her for it.

I remember the week before the 4th of July holiday, 1961. I was as big as a house by this time and could hardly get up and down, but I went into the store and sat on my butt and packed 50,000 worms! That was my last job at the store until many months after Scott was born. (If someone would have told me years before that I would be making a living counting and selling worms, I would have told them they were crazy.)

I was now 45 pounds heavier than I had ever been in my life. I could hardly walk to the backyard, and sit under the grape arbor Dad had made many years before, without huffing and puffing. It was terribly hot and my feet were starting to swell. The Doctor was concerned about my heart being too overworked. He ordered lots of rest and told me to stay off my feet. Mother would bring a tub of water out for me to put my feet in. Otherwise, I really had a good pregnancy and had very few bad days.

We were all anxiously awaiting this baby. My brothers and sisters-in-law visited quite often and were very supportive of my elephant-sized body — they kept teasing me about having twins. My cousin Walter Dailey, his wife Myrtle, and son Rick came up from Florida the last week in July and told me they "...weren't going home until you have that baby." Our baby-to-be would probably be the last baby in that generation. Glen and Esther's son, Barry was nine years old (he was a Down Syndrome child whom we all loved). Now our baby would be the latest toy for everyone to fuss over and play with.

At times I was concerned about my baby. Why did God wait so long to give us another baby? I would soon be 36 years old and was about to bring a new life into the world. Would it be normal and healthy? Would I be too old for it in a couple of years? Would I have a good delivery? (Well, God, there is a reason for everything — so I will leave it in your hands.)

On August 5, 1961, at 7:35 a.m., Scott Harry Stokes, our perfectly new baby, made his grand entrance. What a beautiful baby he was! When the nurse held him up for me to see, his shoulders were broad and tapered down to his round buttocks, with his little testicles bulging through his little fat thighs. I cried, "It's a boy!" He then started to cry as the nurse was cleaning him up and I said, "My gosh, he has a big round mouth." I was afraid he would have marks on his face, like Gail had from the doctor using forceps, but he didn't. I was exhausted but I did have a good delivery even though he was a big baby. He weighed 8 pounds 4 ounces. I had an excellent obstetrician, and the doctor who gave me the "caudal spinal" knew what he was doing.

What a happy Dad Harry was! He went home to tell everyone that baby boy was fine and so was momma, then he went down to the store and changed the sign on the marquee to read: IT'S A BOY!

The Stokes family now had two boys to hopefully carry on the STOKES name. Harry's older brother, George (and wife Peggy) had three daughters and one son, plus another girl was

Dad, Mom, and Scott at 18 months—at the backyard
swim club at 909 Butler Pike, Ambler

143

born just three months after Scott arrived. So Pop and Nannie Stokes now had seven grandchildren, 5 girls and 2 boys.

Nannie Stokes was in and out of the hospital a few months before Scott was born; but she died in April, 1962, not knowing her last two grandchildren very well.

Chapter 14

"DYNALLOY BELLE" AND WORMS

Harry's mother, Nannie Stokes, was born into a family late in life so, as a result, her sister was 18 years older. So Nannie was catered to and pampered quite a bit as she was growing up. I also presume she had a good head on her shoulders because she moved to the Philadelphia area and was Head Buyer for Chatlins Department Store in Norristown before and after her marriage to Pop Stokes.

Now Pop Stokes was raised in a family with five sisters and one brother. I believe his father died at an early age, leaving the mother with these children to raise and, as a result, Pop Stokes was taken out of school and put to work at the tender age of 10. He was sent out to Michigan to Chrysler Corporation and was taught to be an automobile mechanic, which he did for many years. Later in life he became an excellent lathe operator.

Pop Stokes was the most gentle, loveable man I have ever known in my whole life. He was always happy-go-lucky and fun to be around. (That's where Harry got his good nature from.) When he was a young man living in Philadelphia, he was an end man in a minstrel show, and that's where Nannie met him. She went to these shows quite often to watch this particular end man, and got up enough nerve to go backstage and talk to him. About five years later they were married.

A short time after Nannie Stokes died in 1962, Pop Stokes retired. He was a man who liked to keep busy, so Harry opened a bicycle repair shop in our store just to give him something to do.

Also about this time, a customer came into the store from Norristown and told Harry there was a sightseeing boat for sale

at Haws Avenue. He asked him if he would be interested in buying it. Harry said, "I don't have time for a sightseeing boat. I
don't have enough hours in the day now." But as usual, Harry
started thinking about this deal, and thinking it might be a way
of making some extra money. (Here we go again into another
one of Harry's opportunities.)

So he bought the boat and made Pop Stokes Captain of the
"Dynalloy Belle." It was a 40-foot paddlewheel boat with a Dodge
motor taken from a Chrysler car. With Pop Stokes' knowledge
of Chrysler motors, it was well-maintained. We had lots of fun
over weekends taking friends and relatives for rides. It became
quite a conversation piece as people came to watch Pop Stokes
take on passengers for a sightseeing trip up and down the
Schuylkill River.

One of the highlights at that particular time was that some
dignitaries were brought to Norristown on the "Dynalloy Belle"
to inspect the river and also to have dinner at the Norristown

The Dynalloy Belle had to be scrapped following the flood of 1973

Yacht Club. Senator Richard Schweiker was among this group of men, so Pop Stokes felt quite important.

This new venture with the "Dynalloy Belle" put another strain on our marriage. We were too busy at the store, plus church. Now being owners of a boat, especially this type of boat meant a Captain's License had to be obtained. This meant Harry had to study, plus take courses on navigation. If Pop Stokes were to take people on excursions up and down the river, he also had to pass a navigations test.

Harry and Pop Stokes went to Philadelphia to the Naval Yard to take the test. Harry passed right away, but Pop didn't understand the written questions. As a result, he had to go back two more times. Finally, Harry said to the fellow who was giving the test, "Could you ask my Dad these questions verbally, because I know he knows them. It's just the way they are written that confuses him." As a result, Pop Stokes passed and got his Captain's License too.

So Pop Stokes was made Captain of the "Dynalloy Belle." This gave him something to do. Although the bicycle repair business was good, it got to the point where we didn't have enough room in the store for the parts — therefore, Harry phased out the bike shop.

Pop Stokes handled the death of his wife, Nannie, very well and, in time, left Norristown and moved into a lovely apartment in a private home near us in Ambler. With Dad and Mom living with us, we didn't have an extra room. George and Peggy Stokes now had five children so their house was full too. We all took turns cleaning his apartment. In fact, Gail and Peggy's girls took turns on Saturday cleaning for Pop Stokes. I did his laundry, so he was well taken care of. He would eat a lot of his meals with us. We loved him very much.

Scott was a toy for him and everybody else. Pop Stokes would put Scott on his knees and sing a song, "...eep, ipe, a huckleberry pie...", and he would make gestures with his hands to make Scott laugh. When he would finish the song, Scott would say, "Pop, do it again!" All the grandkids remember him for this. He was always happy.

When the "Dynalloy Belle" began taking up a lot of his time, he was spending less time in his apartment in Ambler and more time in Norristown along the river. So eventually he moved into the Blackfan Apartments in Norristown, which was owned by Peggy Stokes' father. When the "Dynalloy Belle" had to be put in dry dock for the winter, Pop Stokes didn't have too much to do, so he would do some errand running for Harry.

Pop Stokes had three maiden sisters — Charlotte, Louise, and Mary — who had just moved to Ocean City, New Jersey. He would go visit them and stay for a few days at a time. The sisters hadn't lived in their new home very long until Aunt Mary found out she had cancer. Not wanting to be a burden to Aunt Charlotte and Aunt Louise, she went into the garage, sat in the car, turned on the ignition, and asphyxiated herself. This was quite a shock to all of us and, as a result, Pop Stokes spent even more time with his sisters in Ocean City. Just a year later, Aunt Louise died with cancer. Aunt Charlotte was alone now, so she asked Pop to move in with her.

Scott was now growing into quite an active young boy. He would follow my Dad all around. When Dad would go to the garage, which he had turned into a carpenter shop, Scott would walk behind Dad with his hands behind his back and try to walk in Dad's steps. He couldn't do this, because Dad had a long stride with his six-foot frame. Mom was watching out the kitchen window and said, "Look at that boy trying to walk in his grandfather's footsteps." We both got a good laugh about that.

Scott, being the last of that generation, and also the baby, got more love and attention than all the rest put together. My oldest brother, Alvin, would come down to our house almost every Saturday to play with Scott, and would sometimes take him home with him for the day. I tried to spend a lot of time with Scott because again, even though Harry finally had a son, he didn't spend as much time with him as I thought he should. Scott was a very pleasant child, the same as Gail was at that age, but he got more attention. There were 10 1/2 years between him and Gail, so he had three mothers — my Mother, Gail, and me.

I would like to inject a few stories at this time about Scott. We had new neighbors — Boots and Eleanor Schrack — who had moved in next door to us, and they idolized Scott. Before we had a gate, Scott was playing in the backyard one day and began wandering down the driveway, getting closer to Butler Pike, a busy road. When our neighbor saw how close to the road Scott was, she said, "You better come back here; you might get hit by a car." I was coming out of the door and heard Scott answer, "Eleanor, go in your house and mind your own business." Well! Needless to say, a little boy got a few swats on his fat little butt for that one. (And we are still good friends to this day with Boots and Eleanor, especially Scott.)

Another time, I had just come home from grocery shopping and had Scott with me. I pulled up along the patio where the front door was. I put Scott inside the door and told him to play while I unloaded groceries. Our house was off of Butler Pike. As I proceeded to take in the last bag, I looked down the road and noticed all the traffic was stopped. A lady got out of her car and started walking up the driveway, holding Scott by the hand. He had wandered out into the street. I ran and picked him up and started scolding him, never thanking the woman for her kind deed. (Dear lady, I will pause to thank you now — you were an angel.)

When Dad heard about this incident, in a few days a large gate was put across our driveway. That gate was a pain in the neck, because we had to get in and out of the car every time we entered or backed out of the driveway! (What a sacrifice just for an active little boy!)

Now that we knew our little boy was here to stay, I tried to talk Harry into taking out an insurance policy for him, so we could put it towards a college education. Finally he agreed. When the insurance man came around, he said that by the time Scott became college age, it would cost $20,000 to put him through. That statement was made in 1963, and he was right. (Now, in the 1990s, it would cost three times that much.)

We were still very busy at the store and also at church. We did a lot of entertaining and, with Mom and Dad around, our home was always busy with family.

My niece, Barbara, had married Bill Kuhns in 1963, and later that year they were baptized into the Brethren faith. Dad always did a lot of discussing with his grandchildren about responsibilities when a couple is put together starting a new family, just as he did with us kids, so I suppose some of it rubbed off on them.

My brother Glen's daughter, Carol, got married in June 1962, and soon they were expecting their first baby. Glen and Esther would be grandparents, Dad and Mom would be great-grandparents, and I would be a great-aunt. (Boy, how time flies!)

Glen's wife, Esther, was raised in the Lutheran faith; as a result, Carol was raised a Lutheran. Remember in my early writings I said all my brothers went to church after they were married, but they never got involved with church activities. Well, Glen and Esther lived in Lansdale, where the Lutheran church was. As Carol got older and more involved with youth groups and activities, it was only right for her to join this church. Again, I must say it is usually the Mother who directs her children in religion so Esther, being the stronger churchgoer, had this influence over Carol. Glen and Esther took turns going to each other's church. But as time went on and they got older, it was easier to go to the Lutheran Church in Lansdale, as opposed to driving to the Ambler Church of the Brethren.

We were still very busy at the store and with church work so, as a result, we did not see too much of Harry. By now, I was mostly the pickup-and-delivery girl for the store. I could take Scott along with me so Mother didn't have him all the time, but you must know that Scott was never too much trouble for Mom and Dad.

Scott was now 4 years old, soon to be 5 in August. I noticed how Mother kept walking after him, dressing him, tying his shoes, and picking up his toys. Finally one day I said, "Mother, you are spoiling that boy rotten. He won't know how to do anything for himself if you don't quit walking after him." She said, "That's what grandkids are for." (Well, I guess you know I didn't win that one.)

I have to inject a story from that time. When Scott was about 3 years old, he was playing in the backyard with a little dog that one of Harry's customers had given him. Later, when Scott and the dog came into the house, we noticed that the dog was all wet and so were Scott's feet and legs. Then all at once, we became aware of this ungodly smell, like something dead. I said, "What were you doing in the yard?" Scott said, "Bathing the dog in the hole in the backyard." I said, "Take me out and show me."

We went outside. There, just a few feet behind the garage was a water hole, about three feet wide and about one foot deep, with thousands of dead worms in it! (Need I say anything more?) Mother grabbed Scott and I grabbed the dog and we put them both into laundry tubs to scrub them down.

It turned out that Harry had dug this hole several months before (never telling us) and buried these worms, hoping to save them for Spring and hoping they would increase in number. Well, we had a few days of hard rain and, of course, not enough drainage, so all the worms had drowned. That was the end of Harry's worm farming!

And, believe it or not, that was the second time Harry had tried to keep worms. The first time was about five years earlier, back in the winter of 1959. Each day when I came home from work, as I opened the kitchen door, I noticed an awful smell. This was unusual because Mom was always baking or cooking so the kitchen always had a good aroma, but for some reason the good aromas were being overpowered by this repugnant smell. I decided to check it out and said, "Mom, there sure is a rank smell coming from the cellar. I'm going to go down and check. Maybe there's a dead rat between the walls." We had two rooms in the cellar, with a cold storage room behind the furnace wall. As I opened each door, the smell got stronger. When I opened the second door (to the cold storage room) the stench was so strong, it gagged me. I took a quick look at the floor of that room and there, jelled together, were thousands and thousands of dead worms!

I ran up the steps and telephoned Harry, saying, "When did you bring those worms into the cellar?" He said, "Last October, why?" I said, "You get right home and clean up this mess, because Mom and I won't touch it!" I was gagging to badly I ran upstairs to get away from the smell. When Harry came home, he went down to the cellar and came up gagging too! It took him the rest of the day to clean up that mess.

What had happened was that, when he put the worms into the cold storage room, he forgot to check them to see if the overhead light was on. As a result, the light burned out, causing the worms to crawl out of the boxes to look for food. Soon they died. He never told us he had put the worms into the cellar because he knew we would have a fit, so he must have done it one day when we were out!

Anyway, after that episode in 1959, and then the later episode with Scott-and-the-dog-and-the-worms, Harry finally realized that worm growing wasn't a successful part of his endeavors.

Chapter 15

LOSING MY FATHER

When you have an extended family, there are always lots of activities going on. My niece, Carol, and her husband, Bob, had their baby boy. And another niece, Barbara, and her hubby, Bill Kuhns, presented us with another baby boy born February 14, 1965. So our family was growing quite nicely, but soon we would have to deal with sorrow too.

My brother, Alvin, and his wife, Veron, were taking Dad and Mom with them for a vacation back to Bedford County, PA. It was 1966, and they were to pick Dad and Mom up at our house on Saturday morning, September 10th. Alvin pulled into the driveway and Mother started out with the suitcases to help load the car. Dad said, "I want to go to the bathroom and I'll be right out." We had a powder room just off the laundry room, which was very convenient for us all — we didn't have to go upstairs all the time.

I had said goodbye to Dad and Mom the night before, because I didn't want to get up so early and, secondly, because I was still recuperating from a slight heart attack I had over the Fourth of July weekend.

When Dad didn't come out as soon as she thought he should, Mom went into the laundry room to check on him, and there lay Dad — Dead! He was on the floor, lying in a fetal position, with a hand towel still clutched in his hands.

Again when Harry was needed, he wasn't around. He had gone on a fishing trip to Canada the week before, and he wasn't expected to be home until the next day, Sunday. We called our Doctor and good friend, Doc Wiley, and he came to the house to pronounce Dad dead. We didn't move him from the laundry room until Doc got there.

Alvin and Veron went home to call my brothers and families. Gail and Doc Wiley carried Dad's body into the living room and laid him on the davenport — I couldn't lift because of my heart. Mother had gone upstairs to put the suitcases away and also to be with Scott. What a shock to us all.

Dad was only 73 years old. He had complained about different parts of his body hurting over the last few years, but he was never sick enough to be in bed. He just kept tinkering around in the shop and would let Scott use his tools — he had bought a little carpenter set for Scott's Christmas gift the year before and had shown Scott how to hold the hammer and saw. In fact, one day Mother and I watched in the shop window, and there was Scott with his hammer, pounding nails into a piece of wood Dad had given him. Now, this would be all over. We laid Dad to rest in the Church of the Brethren Cemetery, Butler Pike and Hagues Mill Road, in Ambler.

I can remember back to just a few years before Dad's death, we were talking around the table as we always did, when Dad said, "Ruth, do you think you will ever move to Bedford County?" I said, "No, I doubt it with our business and all of my brothers and families here, I don't see why. Why do you ask?" He responded, "Well, Mother and I have been thinking if we die, we will be buried in the Old Mock Cemetery with the rest of my family and your little sister, Flora May. We know it would be an inconvenience for you children, and also with no other family back there, doubt if you would visit very often." I said, "You are right, Dad." He said, "Well then, that settles it; we'll make arrangements to be buried here in the Ambler Brethren cemetery." (We did not realize how soon the time would come for Dad to lie at rest at that site.)

Dad had enough insurance money to pay for his funeral, so there were no outstanding expenses to be a hardship for Mother. Mother handled the death of Dad quite well. Being a strong person plus her strong faith, and also living with us, she kept busy.

Along with the sorrow, I would like to inject a little humor. The morning Dad died, he must have taken his false teeth out of his mouth and put them into his sweater pocket. When the funeral director, Walter Shaeff, came to take Dad's body, he

154

asked if Dad had false teeth. I said, "Yes." Well, he noticed they weren't in his mouth, so he advised, "Don't worry about them now, just bring them along when you come to make arrangements. Gail and I looked high and low, not wanting to bother Mother with this matter. Maybe he put them into a drawer in his bedroom, but they weren't there. Maybe on the windowsill in the laundry room (which he did quite often, and made Mother mad), but they weren't there either. Well, what we think happened when Mother found Dad on the floor, she just automatically went through his pockets, threw the teeth into the waste can without thinking, and they were thrown away. As a result, Dad was buried without his teeth. (They were always a nuisance to him anyway, so why not rest in peace!)

Dad's hand-written will was located in a sealed envelope, labeled *"This envelope Not to be Opened Till My Death. —John Irvin Rogers"*:

"North Wales, Pa. January 27th, 1951

This is My Prayer and Last Will. Time is but a winters day, it is winging me to My Eternal home, this world is Not My home, therefor whatever I possess in Material things, I leave to My Wife Minnie Etta Rogers.

My signature, John I. Rogers.

This is the text for my funeral. 119th Psalm verses 10 and 11 (Thy word have I hid in my heart), verses 30 and 31, verses 63 to 71, and 72.

John I. Rogers

Please, I want a plain laying away when my life's work is ended and my soul has left the body, for it is only clay and dust to dust.

To all my children, I have lived for their souls. I might have made mistakes (but with good intentions), I have tried, the flesh is weak, but we have an advocate (Jesus Christ Our Savior) to intercede for us.

To all my children, read the 16th Chapter of St. Luke and study it, and the Whole Bible, and teach it to my grandchildren. For one cannot come back from the Dead to change the lives of Men and Women.

*To you, Mother and Companion, I have lived true to you
since God joined us together in matrimony, and never will-
fully kept any secrets from you. May the Grace of God keep
you (Dear) and all of our children and grandchildren is my
last prayer. AMEN.*

John I. Rogers

This was my first experience at losing a parent. When Nannie
Stokes died, I felt a hurt and grieved, but not as deeply as I did
for Dad. He had given me life through Mother. He had clothed
me, he had taught me patience, he had reprimanded me, he
had taught me religion, but most of all he had loved me and was
always there when I needed him. Now all those things were mine
to be cherished and for me to hand down to my children. What
a heritage! (Thank you, God, for my loving father!)

Life is death, death is life, so all continued with our daily
duties. Scott became Mom's pride and joy for sure. He was actually a godsend at that time in Mother's life. And we were busy
as usual with the store, home, and church.

Scott began asking questions about his Pappy, such as, "Is
my Pappy ever coming home? Is he in heaven? Can't I ever see
him again?" This was also a traumatic time for Gail, being a
very sensitive person. I had a lot of talking and explaining to
do. As always, I was the one who had to try and keep the household on an even keel.

Harry was growing in his faith so, between the two of us and
Mother's beautiful ways, our life continued on to the next encounter — a decision that had to be made in a few months.

Chapter 16

OPEN HEART SURGERY

Remember in the last chapter when I said I was recuperating from a slight heart attack? Let me go back to that story. Well, it was 1966 and the Fourth of July weekend was coming up, so we were extremely busy at the store. Harry called and asked if I could go pick up worms at Worthington's, as he and the fellows at the store were too busy to find time to go. I went to the store to get the station wagon — it had air-conditioning — therefore, the worms wouldn't spoil in the hot weather.

When I got to Worthington's, he asked, "Where is Harry?" I said, "Too busy to come." He said to me, "So am I; I don't have enough help to load you, so I guess you'll have to do it." So I got to work. About the fifth box of worms that I lifted into the station wagon, I felt something pull at my heart. As I continued lifting boxes, I started to sweat and get dizzy. I finished loading and went over to pay Mr. Worthington. He looked at me and said, "Are you okay? You look pale." I said, "I'm okay; I'm just hot from lifting those boxes." I remember getting into the car and sitting a little while and then continued on to the store.

When I got to the store, Harry came out and said, "Why are you sitting there?" I said, "I'm sick; I think I'm going to faint and also throw up." He said, "It's just the heat; why don't you go home and lie down awhile because I'll need you later on." When I went home, Mom saw me getting out of the car and noticed I was staggering. She came running out to help me into the house and said, "What's wrong?" I said, "I feel like I'm going to faint and I feel like I'm going to throw up. My heart is beating funny."

She helped me to the davenport and said, "I'm calling Doc Wiley. I never saw you look like this before." When Dr. Wiley came and checked me, he said, "You had a heart attack. You

157

should be in the hospital." I said, "What would they do?" He said, "Give you medication and lots of bed rest." I said, "Can you give me medication if I stay home and rest?" He said, "Yes, if you agree to stay in bed." Mom said, "I'll see that she does." So I did. I stayed in bed from July until October — I could go up and down stairs once a day.

By November I was strong enough to go to the store a few hours a day, but no lifting. By that time the Doctor was trying to convince me to have the open heart operation. Boy, did that bring back memories! I told him about my experience when I was young, having to make a decision about a heart operation. Now I was 41 years old — a wife, a mother, and a business partner — and had to make a decision of that kind again. At that stage of my life, it would take a lot of soul-searching and prayers.

One Sunday morning after church, Mark Waltz came up to me and said, "I was talking to Harry and he said that your doctor would like for you to have heart surgery." I said, "That's right." He said, "Is your doctor a heart specialist?" I said, "No, he is just an M.D., but he will suggest one when I'm ready." He said, "I have a brother-in-law who is a heart specialist at Abington Hospital. How about if I set up an appointment with him in January for you, and let him tell you exactly what's wrong."

Scott had turned 5 years old, a month before Dad died. We had enrolled him in a nursery school the year before, so he could be with other boys and girls his own age. The private school was across our street and over a little creek, which spread into a large open field with a stone barn and a large-windowed building which was a classroom. The most remarkable thing about this school was all the live animals — sheep, goats, rabbits, dogs, cats, gerbils, white mice, ducks, chickens — all around the outside field for the children to touch, feel, and ride.

The lady who owned this school was Miss Manley, a gem. She taught the children in the classroom educational things, but most of all she used the animals as things of pleasure for feeling, holding, and loving. She was way before her time. The kids just loved her. The best part of the day for the children was after lessons, when they could go out and play with all these live animals and play creatively.

In order for Scott to get to this school on foot, Dad had built a bridge across the little creek, so he wouldn't have to go another block out of his way. Dad would walk him across the street and watch for him to return home safely. (Aren't Grandads great!)

That Christmas season of 1966 was a bit sad because Dad was no longer with us. We also had this heart problem of mine to face in the future. Again, I knew we had no hospitalization or insurance, so that decision had to be met prayerfully and with an open mind. At the dinner table one evening, during Christmas week, I told the family I would like to be examined by this heart specialist and find out exactly what was wrong with my heart and just what could be done.

My appointment with Dr. Bernard Kinlaw went very smoothly. Within five minutes of testing me he said, "You have a problem with your left ventricle, the duct didn't close after birth. It can be operated on. It's called a "patent ductus." What can be done is you will have to be opened up and this hole will be sewn together or patched like an inner tube. It's a simple operation. When do you want to have it done and at what hospital?" I said, "Pretend I'm your sister; where would you send me?" Without blinking an eye, he said, "Einstein Medical Center in Philadelphia. I think they have the best heart team around."

So things started happening quickly. At the end of January, 1967, I was taken to Einstein Hospital by Harry to meet the heart team and also to have my heart catheterized. I was in the hospital one week and then was sent home to rest until I would be called for the operation. I was told by the heart team that I had to have 10 pints of blood for this operation. If I could get donors, it would help defray expenses. Well, when our dear friends at church heard I needed blood for this operation, my quota was filled in no time. Again, our church was in back of us throughout the whole traumatic experience.

Now I must inject at this time that Harry didn't want me to have this operation. After many hours of talk and prayerful nights, I shared my feelings with Harry. I told him that I couldn't go through the rest of my life lying in bed being a burden to my family, plus watching the children growing into young adults with an ailing mother, not being able to run and play again.

159

"No, Harry, I'm going to put my life into God's hands and, if He wants me to be of any use to you and the family, He'll take care of me." Harry shook his head and said, "You always were stubborn so, if it's your wish, I'll stand beside you!"

Mother was 74 years old that February, 1967. Was I taking her for granted? Was I putting too much on her? What if I died? Could she handle my two growing children plus Harry? Decisions! Decisions! My faith was now being tested again. I did a lot of soul-searching, praying, and reading the Bible. I spent as much time as I could with Scott and Gail (especially Gail who had just turned 16 years old in February). I shared with her the responsibilities she would have if anything happened to me, but she assured me that nothing was going to happen. What faith she had in me!

I remember our minister, Don Rummel, visiting me one afternoon before I went to the hospital. I was sharing these things with him and he said, "God works in mysterious ways. Why don't you leave it up to Him?" At that time, Don and I talked about the newness of life and, with Spring right around the corner, I told him I would be his subject for Easter "the newness of life," because in a couple of weeks I would have a new heart and then a new beginning. The operation was scheduled for mid-March.

But it wasn't to happen that way. In preparation for the operation to take place that March morning, the surgeon and all the heart doctors came into my room the night before to check me out and wish me well. Then as the nurse was bathing me and changing my gown, I said, "I have a headache and my neck feels funny." She said, "You are just getting excited about the operation. I'll give you something to relax you."

The next morning I was awakened at 6:00 a.m. by two nurses, one prepping me and another holding two needles. I said, "I don't feel good. My head hurts and I feel tired." The next thing I knew I was rolled over on my side for two shots in my hip. When I awakened a few hours later, I had the heart team and two nurses by my bed watching me and calling my name. I said, "I feel awful. Is the operation over?" They said, "No, we couldn't operate because you have a fever. We have to give you some tests to see what is causing it." I said, "I told the nurse last night I didn't feel good."

For the next three hours I had blood tests taken; my arms were getting very sore. A doctor came in, sat on the bed, and said, "We think you have hepatitis." I snapped, "Where would I get hepatitis unless I got it from your dirty needles." By then I was tired, hurting, and disgusted, thinking everything should be all over only to hear I had hepatitis.

The doctor said, "We would like to give you one more test so we will need one more sample of blood to make sure." I said, "Okay, but no more. If this doesn't prove anything, I want to go home!" They gave me a sedative and, when I awoke, Harry was sitting by my bed. The doctor came into my room to tell us that I had mononucleosis.

I looked at Harry and then at the doctor and said, "That's it! When I was in the hospital for catheterization in January, two of the student nurses had mono." The doctor said, "How do you know?" I said, "Because the two student nurses who were with me at the beginning of the week were sent home with mono. I was told by the patient in the next bed that her husband had mono, so I picked it up here in the hospital." What could he say!

I was sent home with orders not to let any visitors come into my room. Harry would have to sleep in another room. Gail and Scott were not allowed in my bedroom. Mother had to sterilize everything I touched. She would not stay out of the room — said she was too old to get such a thing and, anyway, I needed attention. (Good ole Mom.)

Well, I guess you know my mind was really working now. Questions such as, "Maybe God is telling me I'm not supposed to have the operation. Maybe I'll be a vegetable or I won't be able to function right." Now my faith was being tested again. When Doc Wiley found out I was sent home, he knew I would give him a rough time, so he was prepared for my questions. The hospital called him and told him I had mono, and said to try and keep me in bed, and also not to let me have any visitors.

Well this was very hard for me. I did a lot of reading and thinking. One day when Doc came to see me, I told him I wasn't going through with the operation — that I was going to call it off. He said, "Don't be hasty and make any decisions just yet. You don't feel good. Your body is tired and so is your mind.

161

When you feel better, you'll know when it's time." I looked at him and said, "We'll see."

I had to take medicine to prevent fever from occurring, and drink lots of liquids. Mono is a disease I wouldn't wish on a dog. One day you feel really good, and the next day you walk to the bathroom and it's all you can do to make it back to the bedroom — you are so exhausted. You must remember I had rarely been sick in my life before, so this was very hard for me to accept.

Dr. Wiley told me a few weeks later that, if they would have operated on me, I probably would have died on the operating table. Because of the fever, my body wouldn't have been able to fight back even with blood going through my veins, my heart wouldn't have strength to handle it. So I had to give the heart team credit for stopping the operation. It was a disappointment to them too, but they knew best.

I would like to inject at this time that those doctors who worked with me were friendly, warm, and very knowledgeable. Each one took time to explain to me the procedure they would use, why this, or why that. Also, the heart-lung machine was explained to me: why the lines on the graph were going up and down, what each beep meant. As a result, I knew every procedure they were going to use on me. I was not afraid of the operation but now I had to rest and get my mind and body on an even keel so I would be ready for this endeavor.

Remember when I said I would put my life in God's hands? Well, one day when I was feeling better, it hit me! My gosh, I wasn't waiting for God to tell me what to do; I was telling Him and everyone else what I was going to do! I told Harry that night when he came home from work to call the minister and have him stop over the next day. When Don came by, I told him I was wrong — I wasn't waiting for God's answer, I was telling God what to do!

What a revelation — and I began getting stronger every day after this awareness. I had an inner peace that I had not had since I was sent home from the hospital to rest! Why do we take so many things into our hands, when all we have to do is be patient and wait for God's guidance. He is always there.

By the first week in May I came downstairs and said to Mom, "Well, I feel great so I'm going to call Einstein and have them set up the operation." She looked at me and said, "I knew you wouldn't wait too long when I saw how well you were. You're some girl!" Mother never expressed her feelings to me as to how she felt about my decision, but she knew she couldn't change my mind once it was made up. Harry was hoping I would not go through with it, but again he knew my stubbornness.

On Sunday, May 10, 1967, Mother's Day, with my suitcase all packed ready to go to Einstein Medical Center, I knew this was it. I kissed Gail goodbye that morning before she went to church. Mother had made a delicious breakfast for us, knowing that would be the last good, home-cooked meal I would have for awhile. Scottie came running to say goodbye, and I sat him on the stairsteps and told him I was going to the hospital and he should be a good boy for Nannie. (Why is it at a time like this, your kids always seem extra special?) I didn't want to say too much to him but, as I hugged him extra tight, thought, "Dear God, don't let this be the last time I'll be holding this special little boy who we waited so long to have!" Mother took his hand and walked me out to the car. As Harry put my suitcase into the car, Mother's eyes met mine. Not a tear to be seen as she kissed and hugged me and said, "I know you're doing the right thing." (What strength I got from those words. What a Mom!)

The operation was scheduled for 8:00 a.m., May 13th, 1967. I had asked to have the Brethren anointing service the night before the operation. Our minister, Don Rummel, performed the service with Stan and Helen Davis attending as Deacons. Harry and Gail held my hands during the ceremony. I felt at ease and knew I was ready for the operation. God was by my side and so was my family.

At the closing of the anointing service, Dr. Harry Goldberg and the nurse came in. I introduced them to everyone. They were quite impressed with the anointing service and said they had never seen it before. Also, I was the only Brethren they ever had as a patient. With hugs and kisses and teary eyes, my family and church friends left me so the nurses could get me prepped, sterilized, and wrapped like a mummy from neck to knees in preparation for the next morning. I remember being given two shots, one in each hip. The nurses were talking quietly as I was being put on a rolling bed to the operating room.

The last picture I had in my mind was the faces of my family and the whole congregation sitting in church just the way I had seen them the last Sunday I went to church.

The surgery was to take about four hours; instead, it took six hours. They ran into trouble when the surgeon opened my chest and found calcium deposits in the lining of the tube to be patched or sewn together. It created another procedure they hadn't counted on so, as a result, the operation took longer.

When I awoke and realized where I was, I turned my head to my right with my ear to the pillow and, for the first time in my 41 years, I heard a strong, regular heartbeat, not the "thump, thump, shhhhhh" noise I had heard all my life. With tears in my eyes I said, "Thank you, God, for my new heart!"

The worst part of the recuperation was being hooked up to tubes to all parts of my body, while listening and watching the heart monitor go "beep, beep" with every heartbeat, anxiety building up, praying my heart wouldn't stop beating.

I was in the Intensive Care Unit four days and was glad when I was taken out. I saw a woman die next to me and a man die across the room. (This didn't help my morale at this time.) I was doing quite well, according to the doctor, but had a scare right before I was moved out of ICU.

It was Saturday night and the student nurses were brought in, I suppose to learn, and also to fill in for the regular nurses. About 10:30 p.m., I noticed I was feeling a bit uncomfortable. I tried to get the nurses' attention and noticed a commotion on the other side of the room. Well, this was when this male patient was dying. Apparently they didn't have enough help and, being student nurses, didn't know how to handle the situation. My heart started beating quite fast, my body was getting real warm, and I felt like the top of my head was going to blow out. A student nurse came running, took one look at me, and kept going — I was hoping she went to get help.

Just as I was about to lose consciousness, I felt my body being turned onto its side and a doctor ordering instructions.

This thought went through my mind: "I went through the operation with no trouble and now I'm going to die and I can't even tell Harry why!" What a feeling! As my mind started working properly, I noticed my little Indian doctor, Dr. Nunaz, was by my side consoling me and telling me everything was going to be all right. One of my tubes had worked loose and I wasn't getting enough oxygen to my brain.

I looked at Dr. Nunaz and said, "What made you come to the hospital at this hour of the night?" He said, "To check on my favorite heart patient, YOU." Thank God, because they told me the next day they didn't have enough help over the weekend, and also these student nurses didn't have enough training. When the student nurse saw my condition, she didn't know what to do, and ran for more help. So my little Indian Doctor saved my life! (I have to say at this time that Dr. Nunaz was from India. He was here in the United States to learn and got all kinds of degrees, which I found out later. He had a wonderful sense of humor and a terrific bedside manner. I grew very fond of him.)

The next day, Sunday, my little doctor friend was there to remove all the tubes from my body but the IV. The nurses gave me a bath from head to toe. Boy, what a good feeling! I told the doctor to get rid of the "beep, beep" noise of the heart monitor because "...it's scary listening to that monster 24 hours a day." He said, "We're working on it." I was moved to a semi-private room away from all the bright lights, tubes, and machines of ICU. What a relief! Harry and Gail came to see me that afternoon with flowers, candy, and goodies from Mom. What a reunion! Now I had a whole new life ahead of me, a wonderful family, and friends all waiting for me to come home.

Gail had turned 16 on February 19th. She passed her driver's test but didn't tell me. On the Saturday afternoon before I came home from the hospital, she came strolling into the hospital room with her girlfriend, Donna. I was looking beyond both girls, expecting Harry too. She said, "Mommie, I drove down today by myself with Donna as my co-pilot." I put my hands to my chest and said, "Thank God I have a new heart or I would have a heart attack knowing you were driving down here to Philadelphia by yourself!" What a joy! My little girl was now a licensed driver.

The day before I came home from the hospital, I woke up feeling quite good, then started reliving my whole life leading up to the operation, when my whole body started shaking and soon uncontrollable tears were running down my cheeks. The girl in the next bed called the nurse and she came running to my bed and said, "What's wrong?" I couldn't stop crying. She said, "Let it all out; this has been inside you for a long, long time." I don't know how long I cried, but I know I was exhausted and relieved at the same time. It's called "post-operative anxiety."

My stay in the hospital was drawing to an end. My incisions were healing very well and my mental outlook was excellent. I built up my lungs by breathing into a machine several times a day — when the little ball hit a certain mark consistently, I was ready to go home. I had penicillin shots four times a day and my hips were getting lumpy, so I asked to have the needle put in my arms. I broke out in hives from the shots, so then I was given the medication orally.

The incision on my left side of my body went from the middle of my shoulder, under my left breast, between my fifth and sixth ribs. So I was quite sore and couldn't move quickly. I had a four-inch incision in my left groin which was still tender but, all in all, I was ready to go home. On Wednesday, May 27th, 1967, I was discharged from the hospital. The whole heart team came to my room to say goodbye and wish me well. With tears of joy, hugs, and kisses, I left Einstein Medical Center, holding on to my precious Harry, knowing I had a whole new life ahead of me.

I was exhausted when we got home. My brother, Glen, was waiting with Mother to welcome me home. Glen said, "What a birthday present — my little sister well and home from the hospital." What a reunion! How good the house looked. I slowly walked through all the rooms, turned around and said, "How good it is to be home. I didn't know if I would ever see it again."

My recuperation went very well. In six months I was doing things I wasn't supposed to be doing, but I felt good, so there was no holding me down. When you are in a hospital or in bed resting as much as I had been during the past year, you have lots of time to think. I was much more aware of feelings, seeing things in a different light. My Christian faith was tested many times within the last year. I realized it was up to me, through God, to build a strong body and mind for the future. Of course, at that time I had no prediction as to what was in store for me.

As I have said many times before, I never knew what it was not to be loved. I received hundreds of cards from family and friends. I had so much company over the weekends, Harry would have to carry me upstairs; I would be so exhausted but happy.

Our household was finally getting back to normal and "celebrity Mom" was able to walk more and drive again. It wasn't long before I would walk to the store and work a few hours a day. I had no restrictions other than to pace myself — if I got tired, I would stop and rest. Also, I was advised to rest every afternoon. I did that for about six months, but then started being my busy self. I did not have to go back to the heart specialist for one year, but I had to visit Doc Wiley once a month just to make sure things were okay.

Doc Wiley wasn't just our doctor, he was our good friend. (I remember the year before Dad died, Scott was up in the shop playing with his carpenter tools when, unbeknownst to Dad, he picked up Dad's small hatchet and was hitting a block of wood. The hatchet glanced off and struck Scott under his knee cap. Dad carried him down to the house and said that the boy had an accident. Of course, it was a Sunday and doctors aren't in. We called Doc Wiley and he said for us to meet him at the office — where Scott had five stitches put in his knee!)

That year, 1967, was quite a challenging one for us as a family, but time marches on and new horizons were ahead.

Chapter 17

SCOTT & POP STOKES

Our baby boy was now going to enter the first grade. With a year of nursery school training plus kindergarten, he was now going on to higher education! Was he ready for this big event? To our delight, he did quite well — he caught on very quickly. Dr. Seuss books were very popular at the time and he had an older sister who would read to him and a Grandmaw at hand all the time. He could read, write his name, and color very well. The first grade was no problem for him. His biggest problem was his Nannie walking after him, waiting on him hand and foot. Since the death of Dad, Scott and Gail became Mom's "everything."

I had the shock of my life when I went to my first P.T.A. meeting representing my son. As usual, I went to all P.T.A. meetings by myself because Harry was always too busy. As I sat in the meeting, I realized I was probably one of the oldest parents sitting there — all these young mothers and husbands were in their 20's and 30's, and here I was forty-two! Boy, did I have to be on my toes to keep up with these young people, and especially with my son! When I shared this with Harry later that night, he said, "Scott's going to keep us young." I thought to myself, "Isn't that why I had my heart fixed? So I could play ball, swim, and run after this active young boy!"

At the end of Scott's second year of school, I came home from the store one day and noticed Scott sitting on the patio with a hammer. I said, "What are you doing?" He answered, "Knocking out my front teeth." I grabbed the hammer and said, "Why would you do that?" He said, "All my boy friends at school had theirs out and I wanted to look like them." What a price we pay for being parents! His hammering wasn't too powerful because his teeth were still in place. He was an August baby and, physically, it made him six months to a year younger than most of his school buddies — but not mentally. By the third grade his teeth came out of their own accord. Now he found out he was just like the other kids.

It was 1968 and we had another heartache. Pop Stokes called me from Ocean City, New Jersey, and asked if I could come down for a couple of days while he had some tests taken at the hospital. He didn't want Aunt Charlotte to be alone. As usual, Mom agreed to take care of Harry, Gail, and Scott.

When I got to Charlotte's and Pop's home, I noticed the house wasn't as neat and clean as I had always seen it before. As I was unpacking my suitcase, Pop said, "I've been having some trouble breathing and can't seem to get rid of this cough. Charlotte made an appointment at the doctor's office last week. The doctor said that she would like some x-rays of my chest and for me to prepare to stay in the hospital a couple of days. This is why I wanted someone to stay with Charlotte."

The next day I took Pop Stokes to Somers Point Hospital and got him settled in his room. Within a few minutes, he was taken for x-rays. About a half-hour later a woman came into Pop Stokes' room and asked, "Are you Mr. Stokes' daughter?" I said, "Daughter-in-law." She said, "I'm Doctor so-and-so. Will you follow me?" She took me to her office and put Pop's x-rays on the machine and said, "Mr. Stokes' left lung is three-fourths eaten away. Did he ever complain of pain?" I said, "No, Pop never complained about anything." She said, "I don't know how he lived so long!" I said, "What can we do?" She answered, "Nothing, it's just a matter of time."

Pop had to stay in the hospital, so I went back to Aunt Charlotte and told her. Now I had to call Harry and his brother, George, to tell them the sad news. The only time I ever saw Pop Stokes sick was when he had a large portion of his stomach removed some years before, but he got over it quite well. Pop was supposed to quit smoking after the stomach operation, but he never did. Now his lung was almost gone, with not much time to live.

Harry and George came to the hospital the next day to see Pop. I noticed there was an oxygen machine near the bed and said, "Pop, are you using this?" He said, "I had trouble breathing last night so they hooked me up to this contraption." I said, "George, come with me; Harry, you stay with Pop." We went to the nurses station and asked what happened. She said, "He had a coughing spell and couldn't get his breath, so we put him on the oxygen machine. The Doctor will be here shortly." We went back to Pop's room and I noticed how pale and tired he looked, but he was still his jovial self, and he asked for a cigarette. I said, "Pop, you can't smoke in here with this oxygen." He said, "Then take me out in the hall." (If I would have known then he had only a few days to live, I would have lit a cigarette myself and handed it to him — even though I loath them.) Harry never smoked, but George did.

Pop seemed to be holding his own, so Harry and George went back to Pennsylvania, with mixed emotions, but both had jobs to take care of. I went home to Charlotte's house to fix dinner for us. She didn't go to the hospital at all to see Pop and, as I look back on it, I think she had some intuition that he would never come home. She would be all alone for the first time in her life!

That evening as she was getting ready for bed, she called me into her room. She was having trouble putting her nightie on and I noticed she was shaking. I said, "Don't you feel good?" She said, "I think I'm going to throw up." Just as I was about to run for a towel, she did throw up. It splattered all over the wall and, to my astonishment, was mixed with a tremendous amount of blood. I thought, "Oh my God, something broke in her stomach."

I settled her into bed and said, "I'm going to call the doctor." When I got the doctor on the phone, I explained what happened. She said, "Take her to the hospital." Well, here I go again. Charlotte already had her nightie on, so I put her bathrobe on, found her pocketbook, and off to the hospital we went. Here I was, making decisions on my own — hoping I was doing the right thing. I stayed at the hospital all night. When I knew

Charlotte was taken care of, I went back to the house to rest a little before calling Harry and George, again!

On the way to the hospital, Charlotte had begged me not to tell Pop she was in the hospital — she didn't want to worry him. So now I was going back and forth from one hospital room to the other. I did not tell Pop that Charlotte was on the next floor below him. Pop's color was now ashen and he had trouble breathing. He had to have oxygen quite often and was getting weaker. The Doctor came into Pop's room and asked me to step out to the hallway with her. She explained to me that Charlotte had stomach cancer and it also would be just a matter of time!

I thought, "Dear God, what am I to do?" Decisions! Decisions! It was too late for prayers of health; I'd pray for them not to suffer! George and Harry returned to the hospital Saturday night. Pop seemed to perk up when he saw them. But we went home from the hospital not knowing what to expect. I was exhausted and was certainly glad I had my new heart — it sure was being used to the fullest at that point.

We went back to the hospital the next afternoon and evening, sharing time with both patients. Charlotte was sedated quite heavily, but she knew who we were. Pop seemed to be holding his own, so George and Harry decided to return home to Pennsylvania. I told them I would stay to see what developed, one way or the other — I wasn't afraid to stay alone. Early the next morning, I got a call from the hospital saying Pop had just died. (I personally believe Pop knew he couldn't get better and, after seeing George and Harry, gave up. What a gem!)

Now, what should we do for Aunt Charlotte? If I didn't stop to see her, she would wonder why. I talked to the doctor and she said, "She can't go home just yet, so you children do what you have to do with Mr. Stokes and we'll handle this end of it." I went into Charlotte's hospital room and told her that I was going home for a couple of days but I would be back. Aunt Charlotte had a niece who lived in New York, and we contacted her. She came to Ocean City to be with Aunt Charlotte until after Pop's funeral.

Pop Stokes died in October 1968, and Aunt Charlotte died two weeks later. Aunt Mary, Aunt Louise, Pop Stokes, and Aunt

Charlotte all died within a few years of each other. What a challenge life is! (They are all sorely missed.)

Time continued on and business was still going strong. We were making a decent living, but Harry still didn't give us as a family much of his time. He was involved with the store, and also very involved with the church. By then, he was involved with District work for the church which took him away at nights. Sometimes he didn't get home until 2:00 a.m. because of the distances he had to travel.

In 1968 our congregation remodeled our church sanctuary and added a new education wing to take care of the overflow and make more room for new activities, hopefully to make the future more viable. Rev. Don Rummel and his family stayed until 1970, and then decided to leave our congregation and move on. So we began looking for a new pastor to step in. The Rummels did an excellent job over the ten years they were with us, but life had to continue on for people of their caliber. Their leaving was much felt by us all but, again, we as a congregation had to stick together and continue the work of the church.

Reverend Jay Gibble was our next pastor to fill our pulpit. They as a family were accepted by the majority of our congregation. It was always rewarding when a new family came into our midst. We as teachers were always ready to accept them because a new person always had something to contribute. The Gibble children were bright and loveable.

Scott was now nine years old, growing very well, and became interested in baseball. We enrolled him in Little League. Being left-handed was an asset to him because all the coaches liked left-handed pitchers. As a result, Scott was picked to be a pitcher. Now, I was quite excited — I had a son playing my favorite sport! Naturally I spent a lot of time teaching him how to throw, stand, and hit the ball. Again, Harry was too busy so I took Scott under my wing.

One evening Harry came up from the store and stood watching my routine with Scott. He said, "He isn't lifting his leg high enough when he winds up to pitch." I replied, "Then you show him how." He did. He watched Scott make a few throws and then went into the house for dinner. When Scott and I came in,

I said, "You know, you could give him a little more of your time."
He looked at me and said, "You are doing a very good job; I'll
take over when he's older."

In one way it was a compliment to me, but in another way it
was a hurt, because Scott needed him all the time, not just
when Harry had time for him. But this was Harry. When he saw
that something was being done, it didn't bother him that he
wasn't part of it. He had so many other interests this didn't
bother him or, if it did, he didn't show it. Scott continued playing Little League Ball until he was twelve years old.

Chapter 18

GAIL ON HER OWN

In June of 1969, we had a high school graduate. Gail was now about to enter the business world with all its splendor and its many doors to be opened, excitement and adventure, that only she could see through the eyes of an 18-year-old. We put a down payment on a new car for her graduation gift — it was a Maverick. She had to pay her own insurance and keep up with the monthly payments. We didn't take any board from her, so the car was her responsibility.

Gail never gave us any problem except for a time in her Junior year of school. She was given the opportunity to go overseas with a group from Upper Dublin High School to tour Europe for four weeks — but she fought it tooth and nail. We had noticed she was getting quite a bit overtaken with a young fellow she was dating quite regular at that time. We thought if she took the trip, her romance might cool off. Also, we were making plans for her to go to dental hygiene school in Philadelphia upon graduation. But she just refused to take this trip. Although we saved $700 and had a happy daughter, we were both deeply concerned for her future.

I would like to inject at this time that Gail worked for us in the store from the time she was twelve years old. She would come in after school and on Saturdays, or whenever we needed her. She learned to count worms, clean shelves, put merchandise away, sweep the floor, and (when she was 14) she was taught how to run the cash register and wait on customers. She really was a great help to us. We noticed we had quite a few more young men customers due to this young lass behind the counter!

When she was sixteen, she came to her Dad one day and said, "Dad, I've been working for you for a long time. I would like to get a job after school doing something else." He said,

174

"Doing what?" She said, "Waitressing. The diner up at Spring House is looking for part-time help and I would like to try it." Her Daddy said, "Okay, as long as it doesn't interfere with your school work." She worked there for a year and a half. As time went on, more hours were being assigned to her and also the lifting of trays and cleaning up was starting to get to her. Finally, one day she said to her Dad, "I think I would rather work for you." So that was the end of her waitressing career.

By 1970, Gail had been out of school one year and was working for a dentist in Jenkintown. She was seeing quite a bit of this young lad, Gary McGinty. One evening just before the Fourth of July, she brought Gary into the kitchen just after Harry and I came home from the store and said, "Dad and Mom, can we talk?"

We listened to these two young people ask for our permission to be engaged, with marriage a year later. But we were not ready for our daughter to enter into this situation at that time. Number One, she was only nineteen; he, twenty. Number Two, he was Catholic, she Brethren. We got into a rather heated discussion, but said if they would wait two years until Gail was twenty-one and they both still felt this way, we would consent.

These two young people had shared their feelings. We as adults didn't seem to understand. In their eyes, we were wrong. They said that we were just trying to keep them apart. (And at that time that's exactly what Harry and I were trying to do.)

At that time we saw something in this young man that we didn't really like — a bad temper. We witnessed a display of this one evening when we were greeting friends at our house for dinner. Gary came driving up the driveway on his way home from work, I suppose to tell Gail something. When she ran out to greet him, she put her hands on his car (which I suppose he had just washed) and he said, "Get your goddam hands off my car!" Our friends were just getting out of their car and asked, "Who was that?" We said, "Gail's boyfriend." As parents, we saw it, but Gail was in love and overlooked it.

Three months later, Harry went off on a hunting trip to Ed Simmers' farm the last weekend in September. When he came

175

home Sunday evening, we had a married daughter. She and Gary had eloped to Elkton, Maryland.

We were terribly hurt. Our only daughter was married by a justice of the peace whom we knew nothing about. Also, her Daddy wouldn't be able to walk her down the aisle. I, as the Mother, not being able to plan a reception and all the frills that go with a traditional wedding. We were crushed!

They had planned it from the night we had refused the engagement — the kids decided to take matters into their own hands. They had rented an apartment a few months before and were furnishing it, so that when they came home from Maryland, they would have a place to stay in case we gave them a rough time. (So they did do some great planning on their own.) We soon found out that Gary's parents had known about this and condoned it. That too didn't sit too well with us at the time.

When she came and got her personal belongings to take to their apartment, I knew we had to accept this relationship or lose her altogether. I wanted to do something special for them that would publicly acknowledge their union.

When we told Jay Gibble about the elopement and our disappointment, he suggested a reception. So we decided to have a surprise reception for them at our church. (Jay had come in as the pastor only a month before, so he was still trying to learn people's names.) The reception went well until Jay said the blessing and forgot Gary's name and used another name; that didn't sit well with Gary. So now we had a married daughter and a son-in-law and, wanting the best for them, we gave our love and support. (Little did I know then that this would turn out to be a successful marriage.)

May I say at this time that there were only two times Gail opposed us. The first time was when she did not want to go overseas in her Junior year. The second time was eloping with this young man that she was so in love with. I realize now that both actions were related to her own feelings. It didn't mean she loved us less, but she wanted to prove she could be herself and make decisions on her own. That much confidence she got from our home training, and now we had to accept her feelings.

I had a few things I wanted to return to the church kitchen a few days after the reception. As I was leaving the church, I noticed Jay sitting at his office desk with his back towards the door. He was typing and didn't hear me come in. I bent over his shoulder, kissed him on his cheek, and said, "Thanks for the splendid job you did at Gail and Gary's reception." He bolted out of his chair like he had been struck by lightning and said, "No one has ever done that before to me." I said, "Oh, that's my way of giving you a special thanks." (Poor fellow, he was new and didn't know that this Ambler Church had a congregation known for its warm affection. Members here were much more than handshakers — we also hugged a lot and kissed a lot. From that time on, Jay did a lot of soul-searching into his feelings too.)

Life continued on for us as a family. Scott had his first encounter with decision-making. He had entered sixth grade and came home from school on the first day saying, "I don't like my teacher." I said, "Oh, Scott, that's because I noticed on this paper you just handed me he's a man teacher." Scott said again, "I don't like him." This was the first time I ever heard Scott so strongly oppose a person. He said that Bill Kuhns and Greg Dummeldinger are man teachers, and they're not like this teacher. Well, I soon found out what Scott didn't like about his new teacher.

I went to the first P.T.A. meeting of the year and met Scott's teacher. He had a pleasing personality, but was very effeminate. When I went home that night, I shared this with Harry. He said, "Do you think he'll be a good teacher?" I said, "I'm sure the School Board must have thought so, or I'm sure they wouldn't have hired him."

The next evening Harry and I talked to Scott about this teacher and told him he didn't have to like this teacher, but he had to respect him for his knowledge, and also give him the chance to prove himself as a human being. Scott did very well that year. As a matter of fact, I think he learned more from that teacher than he did from all the ones he had before. Also, it was quite known that some parents had their children removed from this teacher's class and put into another one.

As a family, it was a growing experience for Scott and gave him an insight into the big, wide world and for the uncertain future ahead of him. We as parents have so much to learn from our children, and this was one experience we felt good about.

Business was going well, except for one on-going argument with Harry. As Spring 1972 was just around the corner, it was my job to see that the Little League uniforms were ordered, that the numbers and letters matched each set, and that I made sure I had someone lined up to sew them. He would bid so low on these orders that most of the time we would wind up just breaking even. It really wasn't worth it. His argument was that these youngsters were our future sportsmen, plus the goodwill might bring in more customers. Well, my argument was when these men who were managers and referees came in to shop, they always wanted everything at a discount, which Harry did, and there went the profit. So it was a never-ending battle between Harry and me each Spring.

It seemed like every year or two we would get involved with a new sport, and in 1972 it was scuba diving. I think we were the first store in the area to sell scuba equipment. We realized if we got into scuba, we would have to know how to work the equipment in order to sell it. Harry, Gail, and I took scuba lessons at a motel pool in Spring House; we knew the owner from his coming into the store.

Again, before selling a product, Harry insisted we learn about it so we could talk intelligently about it to our customers. The three of us enjoyed these lessons. It didn't take long until we could snorkel, breathe with the face mask, and carry the buoyant tank. Joe Thompson, the fellow who taught us, worked at the store a couple of nights a week and all day Saturday. Joe had just returned from service in the Navy and he had a Scuba Instructor's license. He worked in well with this new sports line for Sportsman's Paradise.

This was a growing sport, so now we had to invest quite heavily into this gear because the biggest drawing card was "rentals." Clubs were being formed all around so we had a good following. There is always somewhat of a risk with "rentals," so we always asked for a deposit, with a signature and address, and proof of scuba certification.

We only had one mishap, which was not our fault, but nevertheless, it made us more cautious and very alert to people when making both sales and rentals. This fellow came in for two rentals, and we had sold to him before. Harry said, "You are asking for two tanks; are you going to use them both?" He answered, "Yes, I'm going to Lake Wallenpaupack for the weekend. I will bring them back Monday morning." Well, the tanks were not brought back until Tuesday morning, and not by the fellow who had rented them, but by his father. The fellow who rented them had a friend with him, who apparently had never dived before. As a result of his inexperience, the friend drowned. Our customer who had rented the equipment couldn't face us, and we suppose himself, so he had his father return the equipment. So there again was one of life's hard lessons.

With scuba diving so popular, one divers group was getting together 100 people to go to Hawaii for scuba diving there. Harry and I were invited to go. I was all excited because visiting Hawaii was always a dream I had, ever since I played in Betty Reichenbach's orchestra. We would play all the Hawaiian tunes such as "Blue Hawaii," and "Sweet La Lanie," so now a childhood dream was about to come true.

I came home from the store one night and called my girlfriend, Quinn Beisel, and told her about Harry and me going to Hawaii. She said, "Boy, I wish Gene and I could go! He was stationed at Hickman Field during World War II. It would be fun for me to relive that time there with him." I told Harry about this and he said, "Why don't you find out if the plane is all filled up for the trip." I called the fellow who was putting this package deal together and he said there were still some vacancies. So the groundwork was being put together for the two Beisels and the two Stokes to go to Hawaii. We had one month to get our money in for the trip, scheduled for the last week in March. Well, Quinn and I had a great time buying summer clothes and putting a wardrobe together for the trip.

About a week later Harry came in with tickets to Hawaii and said, "Here you are, Ruth. You and Quinn have a good time!" I opened the envelope and said, "There are only two tickets in here. What are you doing — trying to tease me?" He said, "No, I'm not going!" I said, "Come on, cut it out; where are the other two tickets?" He said again, "I'm not going. I called Gene the other day and told him that I'm not going and he said 'If you don't go, then I'm not going either'". I said, "Harry, why in the world won't you go? It would be like a second honeymoon for us, plus the fact Mother will be here with Scott. We deserve it." He looked at me with his brown eyes shining and said, "I'm afraid to fly!" My mouth dropped; I looked at him and said, "You're not kidding, are you!" (I'd been married to this man for twenty-three years and never knew this about him. I now had two things in my years of marriage to Harry that I had never known about him. One, he was scared to death of hospitals and, two, he's afraid to fly. Boy, life can be full of surprises!)

Quinn and I went to Hawaii by ourselves (this second flight was a piece of cake compared to my first flight in the Piper Cub). We had a very good time. We saw lots of new things and the highlight of the trip was a tour of Pearl Harbor. It was quite heartbreaking to see where so many of our Navy men lost their lives. Hawaii is one of the most beautiful places our country has. The Hawaiian people are so very warm and gentle. The mountains are so full of exotic plant life that it is almost breathtaking. The climate is always warm because of the "trade winds." We had a very enjoyable week, but it would have been even better to have shared this gorgeous place with our husbands!

I would like to share with you at this time about the Beisels — Eugene, Quinella, and son Gerry. Gene Beisel came into our store the first year of our business for a hunting license. When Harry was filling out the license, he noticed Gene was born in Bedford County and said, "My wife and her parents were also from Bedford County." Gene asked, "What is their name?" Harry said, "Rogers." Gene said, "I think I heard my Dad talk of a John Rogers." Later that same night, we got a phone call from an Ed Beisel wanting to visit us. Well, as a result of this meeting, Gene and Quinn Beisel became one of our very closest friends.

Chapter 19

LOSING MY MOTHER

In January 1973, Mother had a slight heart attack and was taken to Suburban General Hospital in Norristown. This was Mother's first experience as a patient in a hospital. She had five babies, but all born at home. Now she was in a hospital being taken care of by strangers. For her, this was as much of a problem as the heart attack itself. She had to be hooked up to a heart monitor, given injections, and be fed intravenously, something so far removed from her lifestyle that it was hard for her to accept. When I went into the ICU room and saw her so helpless looking, I wanted to cry. She reminded me of a frightened child, wondering what all those gadgets were and what she was doing there. She did co-operate, so her stay was not too unpleasant.

About two months before Mother had her heart attack, she cut a cuticle on her right toenail and the toe had become infected. She had tried to doctor it herself. She didn't tell me and one morning I noticed she was limping. I said, "What's wrong, Mom?" She said, "I got a sore toe." I said, "Let me see it." Her big toe was almost black. I said, "Mom, I have to take you to a foot doctor." As usual, she was going to put up a kick, but I vetoed her and made an appointment for the next day. When Dr. Reese saw the toe, he said, "Minnie, why did you wait so long?" She had to soak it several times a day and put medication on it.

It was healing quite well but, when she had the heart attack, the doctor in the hospital didn't do anything about the toe. I happened to lift the sheet from the bottom of Mother's foot to look at the toe. It was swollen and had turned black! I was shocked and said, "Mom are they doing anything to your toe?" She said, "No." I jumped up from my chair and headed for the nurses station with anger in my heart. When I approached the nurse about Mom's toe, she said, "The doctor will be in shortly." I knew there was something wrong by the tone of her voice.

About an hour later I was approached by this doctor to come to the nurses station. When I confronted him about Mom's toe, he bluntly said, "We were more interested in her heart than her toe!" I said, "My God, man, her toe is worse now than when she came in." He said, "We're thinking about removing it and want your consent." My heart started pounding and I was getting a little excited and said, "Will Mom's heart stand an operation at this time?" He said, "I don't know." I said, "Then don't operate." Mother was in the hospital ten days until she could come home. I called the foot doctor, Dr. Reese, the first day that Mom came home from the hospital. He took one look and said, "We'll have to start all over again." So every day I soaked Mom's toe and put medication on it.

On January 22nd, Mother started getting pains around her heart and was very tired. I called Doc Wiley. He came right up and gave Mom a sedative and said, "I don't know how long this will last, so give me a call. We may have to take her to the hospital again." I said, "What would they do for her there?" He said, "Keep her sedated." I said, "Are you telling me Mother is dying? If so, I'd rather take care of her myself."

Mother had a restless night and the next morning Doc Wiley came and gave her another pain relaxer. He said, "Her pulse is getting weaker. I suggest you tell the rest of the family." First, I called Leonard, who was at home recuperating from a stay in the hospital — he was being treated for cancer. The rest of the family was also notified.

Gail was working for the dentist, Dr. Mark Waltz, of Ambler. Lots of days she would spend her lunch hour visiting with Mom and me. This would be her last day to see her precious Nannie alive. Gail was pregnant with her first baby, due in April, and her Nannie would never get to see her new baby!

Leonard came that afternoon to see Mom before she died. It was all he could do to get up the stairs (by crawling on his hands and knees) because he was in such a weakened condition from his cancer therapy treatments. Mother knew who he was, and asked how he felt, but her conversation was slowly trailing off. She seemed to lapse into sleep and then awaken and look at us both, but didn't talk.

Harry came up after Leonard left and looked at Mom and said, "How's my best cook?" Mom gave no response. Scottie came home from school, ran up the steps, looked into Mother's room and said, "Hi, Nan!" as he went to change his school clothes. My niece Barbara Kuhns and her husband, Bill, came to the house as soon as they got off work. She turned her head toward Barbara and I fluffed up her pillows, but she made no response.

Barbara and I were making small talk to one another. We each had one of Mother's hands. Barbara bent down and kissed Mother on one cheek, and I kissed the other. I don't believe ten minutes passed until Mother lifted her head slightly with her eyes closed, took a deep breath, and passed away. She had a very peaceful look on her face. She was now in God's hands.

Although I wanted to be there with her, I had never seen death so close before. So Mother's death was quite a traumatic experience for me. Looking back and reminiscing, I now know it was for Barbara too! Her Nannie Rogers was one of her best-loved persons in her life. Mother practically raised Barbara until she went to school. Barbara was at our house more often than any other nieces or nephews. It seemed when Barbara got sick, her mother Jenny didn't know how to cope with it and, as a result, Mom would say, "Well, let her stay with me." So now this precious love of Nannie's was gone.

The loss of Mother was felt very deeply by all those who knew her. Mother was laid to rest next to Dad at the Church of the Brethren Cemetery in Ambler. Mother died January 23, 1973, on my brother Leonard's 53rd birthday. (We did not know at that time that in only two more months, his body would also be laid to rest near Mother.)

A few years before his death, my brother Leonard had been told he had cancer in his stomach, and that he should quit smoking and drinking alcoholic beverages. Having a "devil-may-care" attitude, he took this information lightly. I personally believe he could have lived longer if he would have listened to the doctors. But realizing what pain and agony he went through before he died, maybe he knew best. To see a loved one deteriorate before your eyes as he did, I was glad Mom and Dad both went the way they did.

Leonard was in and out of the hospital the last few months before his death. His coloring was terrible, he was losing his hair, and he was nothing but skin and bones. The cancer had spread from his stomach to his neck, and finally to his brain. He died in March of 1973. I thought I could hardly stand losing two loved ones within a few months.

Then another loved one died in July, 1973. My oldest brother Alvin (who had been a diabetic for several years), was taken to the hospital with severe pain and died a few hours later. What a sad year that was! I lost a mother and two brothers, but had to continue on as a wife, mother, and businesswoman.

In between two deaths, Harry and I became grandparents. Kelly Jean McGinty entered this planet Easter Sunday, April 22, 1973. We were awakened early Easter morning by her tired, proud Daddy, telling us new Mommie and daughter were doing fine, and he was going home to get some sleep. Gary was Gail's breathing partner throughout the delivery, so this took a lot out of him too!

We went to church that morning and Harry got up and announced that "Ruth Stokes became a grandmother this morning. Mother and baby are doing real good, but it sure was hard on Grandpaw!" Good news travels fast and far, so the birth of our grandbaby was celebrated with cards, flowers, and gifts.

I was with Gail when she came home from the hospital, so I had the fun of changing, caressing, and loving this new little bundle of joy. Scott was an uncle at 12 years of age, so now he had something on his buddies. The last day I was with Gail while she got her strength back, she was watching me diaper Kelly when she said, "Mommie, I can't believe she's all mine and she's so perfect. I only wish Nannie could see her." We both got teary-eyed and I said, "She knows, Gail."

Chapter 20

ARMED ROBBERY

The year 1974 was an interesting, but different kind of year for us. We knew a couple by the name of Silas and Edith Shoemaker who used to go to our church. They lived in Ambler in a beautiful old 1874 farmhouse about two blocks from our home. Now that they were getting up in years and their son and daughter had married and moved away, it was much too big for them. Silas stopped by our home one day while coming from the corner store with a newspaper in his hand and said, "Edith and I are going to look into Peter Becker Retirement Community; we feel our home is too large for us to take care of, and the children live so far away from us, that if we get down sick we would be better off knowing there would be care for us close at hand." In the same breath he asked, "Would you know anyone who might be interested in buying a home of our size?" I answered, "Yes, me."

When Harry came home that evening, I told him what Silas said. Harry said, "Did he say what he was asking for it?" I said, "I didn't ask; I just wanted him to know I was interested." Harry said, "There you go again, getting involved with something when we don't have any money." I said, "Sell this house. We're too close to the street. Besides, we would have a bigger garage to store things in and a more private lifestyle." End of discussion.

A few days later Harry called from the store and said, "Make an appointment with the Shoemakers to show us their house." I had been in their home a few times as a young girl with Dad and Mom. Sometimes the Deacons would have meetings in each other's homes. As a result, I knew this beautiful old country home.

I remember the beautiful large living room, with fireplace, and long French doors that opened out to a pillared spacious porch. So Harry's phone call delighted me, and I also thought, "Boy, he is interested too!"

As the Shoemakers were showing their home, I would watch Harry's face, and I could tell he liked what he saw, especially when he heard the asking price. We went home and started making plans to sell our house. Mr. Costa, who owned a grocery store on the corner of Route 309 and Butler Pike, had bought the house next to his store and our house was next to that. He asked us years before if we ever thought of selling, let him know. Well, the wheels were put into motion. We owed only $5,000 on our house, and Costa wanted our house in the worst way, so things were looking up. We negotiated with him and settled on a price.

A few days later Silas called and said they had been accepted at Peter Becker Retirement Community and they needed to put $10,000 down; could we give that to them as a down payment for their house. Well, here we go again. Where were we going to get $10,000 — we hadn't sold our home yet. Well, remember in an earlier chapter I told you about a friend of Harry's, this bachelor fellow by the name of Ed Simmers? Harry called him and asked him if he could lend us this amount until we sold our house, which was already in progress. A few days later Ed Simmers called and said that he would like to come down the following weekend. Mr. Simmers had leased his property in Maple Glen and bought this farm in Dushore, Pennsylvania, where he intended to remain the rest of his life. (Well, this would change too!)

Mr. Simmers came to our home at 909 Butler Pike in Ambler. He had a briefcase and inside was a checkbook and a revolver — he always carried a gun with him. He was a strange-looking man. He had very thick glasses, gray hair, and broad shoulders that tapered to small hips. He had been diagnosed with throat cancer a year before, so his larynx (voice box) had been removed. This surgery left a hole in his neck. Unable to speak normally, he used a plastic tube and a device that could vibrate against the throat — an apparatus invented for people with this problem: IT-CREATED-A-MONOTONE-VOICE-BUT-IT-SOUNDED-LIKE-A-ROBOT. We got used to his "talker" (as we called it) so we could communicate very well with him.

Lots of people couldn't understand him and this would make him mad. But in our dealings with the public, we had to listen to all kinds of voices and accents. As a result, we felt it was easy for Harry and me to understand this man and his "talker." Harry was already quite close with this man who was about to share some of his hard-earned money which he had acquired by his intelligence and patience. But at one point in his life, a heart attack almost killed him — that's how I really got involved with Ed.

Before he had this land developed for commercial businesses, Ed had been a third generation owner of his home property in Maple Glen, Pennsylvania, and also a third generation Postmaster there. The property had belonged to his Grandfather Simmers and was handed down to his father and upon his father's death, it became Ed's. Ed was an only child who was born blind in one eye and with very little vision in the other eye. He was not sent to school until he was nine years old, because his Mother tried to protect him, but his Father insisted he go. He was sent to a one-room school at Three Tuns. Because he could not see the blackboard, he would memorize all the lessons, including those for the other grades too. As a result, he was ahead of most of the kids in his class and became an ardent student.

He went on to Ambler High School, played football, and to this day has the longest shotput distance ever made at Ambler High. He walked from Maple Glen to Ambler to school, then would come home and work in the family store and Post Office.

When he decided to develop this property for a shopping plaza, he came up against a lot of opposition from Upper Dublin Township. Sewage and water was quite a problem because the sewage lines were not brought out that far as yet, and everyone had their own wells. Ed could see how the outskirts of Ambler were being built up and tried to tell these men on the Zoning Board to "get on the stick" for the future. As a result, a lot of foot-dragging was being done.

Also, a contractor who was building this maze of stores for Ed was stealing lumber and equipment intended for Ed's buildings. Instead, it was being used for a home he was building for himself — and charging Ed for the material. Realizing the bills were much higher than the estimates, Ed found out what was

187

happening. Words were exchanged and with all the turmoil of an upcoming court case, Ed had a heart attack. While Ed was in the hospital, the lawyer representing him died suddenly, so Ed dropped the charges and expelled the contractor who had been taking advantage of him.

When he came home from the hospital, he called Harry, told him he was home, and he was hungry for some apple pie. So I got a phone call from Harry asking me to take an apple pie out to Ed. When I took the pie to Ed's home, his Mother let me in and I went upstairs to Ed's apartment. What a mess! I said, "Don't you have someone to clean for you?" He said, "I-DID-IT-BUT-SINCE-I'VE-BEEN-SICK-I-DIDN'T-BOTHER." At that time his Mother was in her eighties, she couldn't take care of herself properly, and her part of the house was filthy too! I went home and told Harry what I had seen.

The following week I got a lady to clean the house for a couple of weeks, only to be bad-mouthed by Ed. He didn't want anybody in his home; he didn't trust anyone. As a result, he lived in a dirty home which I refused to go to.

When his mother went into a nursing home, Ed finally moved to the farm in Dushore, PA, but I didn't want to go with Harry to see him. Ed did find a country lady to clean his farmhouse, so it was cleaner than his last house. But Ed was anything but refined. He was a crude man with his mouth. And his hygiene was awful — I suppose because he didn't have a woman around, it wasn't always necessary to shave and bathe very often. But I will admit he was always very nice to me from the very first time I met him until he died.

We would get phone calls from Ed a couple of times a week, either at the store or sometimes we would just get in the house at 9:30 p.m. and he would call. I would get aggravated because he would talk at least a half-hour at a time. We would be tired from twelve hours of work; also, it would eat into our private time with the family and each other. Our time was very precious to us. Our relationship as husband and wife was very solid at this time — we grew closer to each other as our family grew. Scott was 12 years old, plus we were grandparents.

Now we had made this decision to buy the Shoemaker's old country home before we really had the money. Our settlement date had not been set. However, the Shoemakers needed $10,000 by September 1st as down payment on their apartment at Peter Becker Community. Knowing we didn't have cash available, Harry asked Ed Simmers to loan us $10,000. He did.

Since our 25th wedding anniversary would be in August, we thought the new home would be quite a gift for us. And Gail kept stopping by and calling, trying to find out when we would be moving into this big country home. (She was trying to plan a surprise 25th anniversary party for us, but not having an exact date for the move was fouling up her plans.) As usual, things fell into place and we moved to 1001 Butler Pike on the Memorial Day weekend, 1974.

But 1974 was another year in which the economy slowed down. Banks were not lending money too freely, and a noticeable economic recession was taking place. I was rather excited about selling our old house to buy the new one, which we could pay off and not have any more mortgage payments. However, I found out that Harry had taken the money from the sale of the house and paid off $40,000 worth of bills he had at the store. Then he went to Norristown Mortgage Company and borrowed money to mortgage our new home — with payments twice the amount we were paying before! I guess you know quite an argument resulted over that situation. As I said earlier, Harry still would not let me get involved in the bookkeeping at the store. Now I was beginning to find out why — he was getting deeper and deeper into debt at the store, and business was slow. Money from the sale of our home was his way out for awhile.

We were still involved at church, plus Harry was on a Brethren District Board. He was taking a lot of his time traveling back and forth, getting home very late at night. He was also starting to get out of breath, and he tired very quickly. I told him to please go to Doc Wiley's for a check-up, but that was like talking to your hat.

Then something devastating happened — there was an armed robbery at our store. In June, 1974, on a Friday evening, Harry, Scott, Norm, and I were in the store, and we had eight customers milling around looking at merchandise. Harry and I were behind the counter. Scott was over by the gun case, and Norm was showing some fishing rods to a customer. I had just

189

looked at the clock and was glad to see it was 8:45 p.m., soon time to close up. Fridays were always busy and this one was no exception.

A customer was paying his bill when I noticed two black men coming into the store — one was carrying a guitar case, and the other had his hand in one pocket. Right behind them were two more men. As they came closer, I noticed one had a pistol in his hand. I stepped closer to Harry as he was making change, touched his leg, and said in a low tone, "One of those fellows has a gun!"

I looked up as the one with the guitar case walked past the counter towards the gun case. The second one went into the scuba department. The third one walked towards the counter. The fourth one went beyond the counter to a customer with three young boys. As each robber positioned himself in the store, Harry reached under the counter and pushed our alarm button. The alarm was hooked up to the State Police in Norristown, the Ambler Police, and our home.

The fellow with the guitar case opened it, pulled out a sawed-off shotgun, pushed Scott down on his knees and told him not to move, then with the butt of the gun broke the glass on the gun case. As he was doing that, the second one came behind the counter, forced Harry to the floor, face down, then put a pistol to my head and told me, "Open the cash register!"

The third robber forced Norm, plus the father and his three small boys to lie down and give him their wallets. One of the boys reached into his pocket and pulled out a quarter — the robber knocked the quarter out of the boy's hand as he was going through the men's wallets. The fourth robber was the lookout man.

The one behind the counter with me was dancing back and forth from one foot to the other, still with the gun at my head. He told the other customers not to move. Everyone co-operated; not one of the little boys cried or hollered (they were between 6 and 12 years old). After the robber took the cash, he told me to get a bag and put ammo in it. (We kept all ammunition behind the counter). As I was putting ammo into the paper bag, I said, "It's going to tear." He said, "Shut up, and keep filling the bag." Well, needless to say, that's what happened. As ammo fell and scattered across the floor, the lookout said, "Hurry up, let's get out of here."

The one with the guitar case was filling it with all the guns it would hold, and also put a couple more under his arm. I could see Scott still lying on the floor and I was praying that he wouldn't try to do something! The lookout kept hollering to get going. The robber next to me had a sweet smell about him, and I can still see those shoes — they were brown and white, with platform heels. The robber with the guitar case came past the counter with his arms full. The one next to me pushed me aside and they all left.

As we were trying to compose ourselves, two cops came through the door with their guns drawn, but they were too late; the robbers had left just minutes before. All this catastrophe happened in about 10 minutes! What a night!

The FBI was called. The agents took lots of pictures, checked for fingerprints, and asked us questions. We were all shown mug shots. Scott, myself, and one customer were the only ones to pick out all four men. When Harry said they all looked alike, one FBI man said, "Don't EVER say that when you're in court!"

The robbers took a little over $5,000. They were a group from Philadelphia who, at that particular time, were trying to build an arsenal and start a black militant organization. Later we learned that one of them was out on bail for murder. Two were over 21, the lookout was 18, and the one with the guitar case was only 14 years old.

A month later two of them were caught while robbing a Wawa convenience store in Spring House — the two youngest. We were called to court to identify the two boys and have them charged with entering and robbing our store. Because they were under 21, and it was a first offense for both, they were sentenced to 3-5 years in jail, but could be out in 2 years for good behavior. (The other two were still not caught at that time.)

Harry called our insurance company to report the robbery, and the insurance man came the following week. Harry told him about the robbery and how much we had lost. The insurance man asked, "Did they break and enter?" Harry said, "No, they walked in with guns, floored us all except my wife, and held a gun to her head." The insurance man said, "You're not covered." Harry said, "What do you mean?" The man said, "They had to break and enter." Harry said, "Do you mean I have been paying into your company all this time and now I'm not going to be compensated because these men didn't break and enter into my store?"

Harry was never a swearing man, but for one brief moment he lost his restraint. He grabbed that man by his coat collar, pulled him halfway across the counter and said, "You son of a bitch! My family, my working man, and myself could have been killed — and you're telling me I'm not covered by your insurance? Get out! Don't ever set foot in here again!" Harry dropped all insurance coverage and never took any out again as long as we had the business. He was bitter and hurt. And just a few months later, Harry had his heart attack. I know in my heart this robbery shortened his life.

The other two robbers were caught and convicted. Scott and I were still going to court even after Harry had died. We never did get compensated for our loss, and we never got our guns back. We were told the guns were taken to the Center City (Philadelphia) Police Department — even though we identified all our guns by the serial numbers after they were confiscated. I suppose, in time, someone else was enjoying what we lost.

Chapter 21

LOSING HARRY

In August 1974, we did have a surprise 25th Anniversary Dinner which was pulled off by Gail and Gary, and our good friends, Gene and Quinn Beisel. We were taken out to dinner, then later brought to the Lansdale American Legion Hall where a gathering of our friends and relatives were waiting to share a good time. It was a wonderful day of fellowship and reminiscing. (No one knew it would be our last anniversary together.)

Scott was 12 years old and it was his first year to go hunting with his Dad, and this meant a lot to Harry. He couldn't wait for his son to be old enough to hunt and fish with him, only to have it so short-lived.

We were all settled into our big, country home (which I named "Rose Hill") and enjoyed sharing it with our friends and relatives. I had a paintbrush in my hands for weeks, getting ready for an Open House the first week in December. I noticed Harry seemed more tired than usual, especially when going up the steps, but he still would not go to the doctor. We were busy at the store, but sales were not as brisk as the year before. At that time of year people would come in to arrange layaways for Christmas, but I noticed a drop-off of sales for this too.

Harry went to the bank to borrow money for our Christmas season, only to be refused. This was the first time this had happened in twenty years. When he asked why, he was told that he was overextended, and the economy was so bad at the time he would be a risk. When Harry came home and told me this, I was shocked. I said, "We'll sell just what we have on our shelves, if that's the case." He just looked at me with hurt in his eyes and said, "We're going to lose the store."

I could not believe things were that bad, but I also hadn't seen the books. I knew Harry kept things from me. I also knew he would borrow a few thousand here and a few thousand there from the loan sharks. This didn't make sense to me because of the high interest rates they charged. When I confronted him about this one day when he wanted me to sign my name for one of these loans, I said, "I'll not sign." He said, "Then you'll be the reason we lose the store." Then I realized he was really in financial trouble. I said, "After the holidays, we'll get to the bottom of this."

We had a wonderful Christmas in our big home. The living room was 18 x 30 feet, with wide window sills and three French doors that opened to a four-pillared porch. So graceful! We bought the biggest Christmas tree we ever had and put it in one corner of the living room. It was just beautiful when decorated. Every Sunday we had company and were always glad to share our home with friends and family.

We got through the holidays, but Harry was really getting tired and was fighting for his breath. I said, "Harry, you cannot keep this up without medical attention." I called Doc Wiley and told him about Harry. He said, "Send him down." But Harry wouldn't go, so Doc Wiley came up to the store. He took one look at Harry fighting for his breath and said, "You have to go to the hospital." What a time to have a sick husband.

It was New Year's Eve, 1974, and Harry was put into the hospital. He had congestive heart failure and was filling up with fluid. I didn't realize at the time he was so seriously ill. Now I had to see about the store, keep house, give time to Scott, and visit an ailing husband in the hospital. (Please God, give me the strength and understanding that I now need.) We did have two good men working for us at the store, Norman Hamilton and Glen Clark. They were both bachelors, not having a family to neglect, and they handled the store very well for me by putting in extra hours. Their time was much appreciated by me.

Harry was in the hospital two weeks without too much improvement, only because his heart was so overworked and his body was run down from all the months of being pushed to its fullest capacity. He had a bad spell one day before I got there and told me he was going to die, that he was tired of fighting to stay alive. A few minutes later, Gail came into the room and he said the same thing to her. She put her arms around him and, with tears in her eyes, said, "Daddy, I won't let you die; you have too much to live for." He looked at us both and asked to be anointed. We called our minister, Jay Gibble. That evening with two Deacons, Gail, Scott, and myself, Jay anointed Harry. After the anointing service, Harry didn't seem quite as restless. We talked a little more and went home. That was the first good night of rest Harry had since his hospital admittance. He was told if he kept feeling better, he would soon be able to go home.

The first of the year was always "Inventory" time, which I hated, but it had to be done. We had lots of good help. When people heard Harry was hospitalized, our phone was ringing off the hook. Also, well-wishers were asking if they could help.

Harry was in the hospital three weeks until he was discharged, being sent home with all kinds of "no-no's" and lots of medicine. He would have to take this medicine the rest of his life to control the fluid and keep his heart on an even keel. He needed lots of rest, which was not part of Harry's makeup. And we had so much company I had to restrict the length of time to the visitors.

Harry never took very much medicine in his lifetime, so it was hard for him to accept this part of his recuperation. I had a schedule made up and the time each pill had to be taken, so I knew just where we stood. One night, about a half-hour after I gave him his last pill of the night, I fell asleep. (I wasn't getting much sleep at that time.) I awoke quickly, though, when I heard Harry walking around the bedroom mumbling and bumping up against the furniture. I tried to get him back to bed, but he just pushed me aside and kept mumbling. I was afraid he would walk out of the room and fall down the stairs. Finally, I got him into the rocking chair and I kneeled at his feet until he fell asleep. When I told the doctor the next day, he said that it was his medication. I thought maybe his mind was going.

We were married for 25 years and this was the first time Harry had ever been in the hospital. He had lots of time to think and also review his whole life. One evening when I came up from the store, I noticed Harry and Scott sitting in the living room talking. This was the first opportunity in Scott's life to have his father with him every day from the time he got home from school until he went to bed. Harry had always been too busy to spend much time with him; now it seemed he didn't have enough. (Sadly, he didn't.)

Harry didn't go down to the store until the first week of March, and then he was restricted to a few hours at a time. This was hard for him to do but he would be exhausted when he came home. I was still going to the store on Friday nights, but was being spared several days a week, this being the slow time of year made it easier.

Our bookkeeper, Helen Leadbeater, was a real gem — I don't know what I would have done without her. By the way, she knew more about the business end of the business than I did at the time. She wrote a lot of checks and deposited bank money for Harry, which at that point I still didn't do. So as a result, she knew where the money was going and where it wasn't.

Harry lost a lot of weight which he should have done years before (but would not listen). He was a great milk drinker, and milkshakes were his favorite snack treat. His friends would tease him about knowing "all the milkshake stands for miles around."

A week later, the second week of March, Harry decided to go see his friend, Ed Simmers, who had called several times a week to see how he was doing, and I suppose had persuaded him to visit. The doctor told him he could go if he got lots of rest and took his medicine. I went along with the idea, only because it was getting harder for Harry to stay away from the store. Spring was just around the corner and all the Spring sporting goods were coming in.

I helped him pack his suitcase and carried it down the steps for him. I was also putting some food and goodies into a shopping bag to take along when he came over to me and said, "Ruth, do you know how much I love you?" I looked at him and answered, "I hope so." He looked at me again and said, "If anything happens to me, will you put Scott into Valley Forge Military Academy?" I just looked at him and said, "I couldn't do that." He kissed me goodbye and went on his way.

I couldn't understand why Harry mentioned Valley Forge Military Academy to me, other than to remember that one time years before Harry said he had longed to go there because of their noted academic standards. We never had any trouble with Scott in school and he seemed to be a good student. He caught on quickly and was alert as to what was happening around him. Also, he was thrown in with adults a lot and could hold an intelligent conversation with anyone. Whether Harry wanted the Military Academy for academic reasons or for their discipline, I will never know!

Harry came home from Ed's house on the 20th of March. I took one look at him and said, "My God, Harry, didn't you take your medication?" His stomach was all bloated and his face was full — I knew he was filled up with water. He said, "I felt so good while I was away; anyway, if I have to take pills the rest of my life to prevent fluid filling me up, I'd rather be dead!" I said, "I'm going to make an appointment with Doc Wiley first thing in the morning."

He unpacked and laid down until dinner. After dinner he said, "I have a meeting at the Gwynedd Valley Sportsman's Club tonight." I would have rather had him stay home, but I knew this meeting was very important because of the "Fish and Pay" weekends coming up before the regular fishing season.

I waited in the TV room upstairs, which we had fashioned from a spare room. Every night after dinner, we would close up the downstairs and spend the rest of the evening watching TV or reading. Also, Scott's bedroom was next door and I could check on him as he did his homework or worked on his car models.

I had just gone over to our bedroom when I heard Harry come in. He came up the steps and into the bedroom with a pleased look on his face and said, "I just resigned as President of the Club tonight. I've been doing a lot of thinking since I've been sick, and decided it's about time someone else took over. This fellow, Max Hesselgesser, is very knowledgeable and I know he will do a good job." (Those were the last words Harry ever said to me.) He undressed, kissed me good-night, and crawled into bed.

I was awakened about 4:00 a.m. by this awful rattling noise coming from Harry. I called his name and, as I turned on the light, I saw he was bluish. I kept calling his name, but got no response. I ran over to Scott's room and said, "I think Daddy is dying! I'm calling Doc Wiley!" Doc got to our home within minutes, took one look at Harry, and started pounding on his chest — but got no response. He looked at me and said, "He's gone."

Scott ran back to his room to be alone. And I just stood there, paralyzed. Harry was only 49 years old; I couldn't believe my eyes! NOW what will I do? I called Gail and Gary, and they were at the house within the next hour. I had to call Helen Leadbeater who came in Friday mornings to do the books and make the bank deposit. I also had to call Norm Hamilton, who worked on Fridays starting at noon. My mind was working overtime, trying to think what to do next. The family had to be contacted. The undertaker had to be called.

Harry didn't like pajamas and never wore them. He said that pajamas got tangled around his legs and twisted around his arm pits, plus he liked the freedom of his body against the sheets. He was a very restless sleeper, jumping and turning all night long. After my open heart surgery, we had gotten twin beds because I couldn't stand his moving around and I was afraid he would hit my incision with his floundering arms.

(I remember one night not too long after we were married when I was sleeping next to Harry. In his sleep, he brought his right knee under my butt and lifted me right out of the bed! As I was lying on the floor I asked, "What ARE you doing?" He looked over the edge of the bed with his shining brown eyes and confessed, "I was running around the bases, and you just happened to be in the way.")

The undertaker, Anton Urban, happened to be a good friend of ours. When Anton came, I was embarrassed when he put Harry into a body bag to carry him out, since Harry didn't have any pajamas on. But Anton said, "Don't worry about it. He came into the world naked and that's the way he went out."

My whole world came tumbling down around me that March 21st, 1975, when I became a widow. I was left with a 21-year-old business which I suspected was in great debt, a 13-year-old son, and a new home with a large mortgage. Boy, was my faith being tested! (Dear God, please help me through this turbulent time. Give me strength and the guidance I need.)

There is no way to explain the death of a spouse. He no longer is here. You wait for him to come through the door, or call on the phone, or hear his breathing next to you, but that is no longer going to happen. It's over; it's done. This man you spent 25 years of your life with — building dreams, sharing ideas, arguing with, laughing, crying, and loving — is no longer part of you. It's like you lost an arm or a leg; you can still function, but it's not the same. Does this feeling ever go away?

The night of the viewing was the most miserable night that God ever made — it rained and rained. But that didn't stop the mourners who came by the hundreds to view Harry and convey their condolences to me, Scott, Gail, and Gary. You never realize how people react to a situation until a time like this. Harry had been a businessman, was very well liked, and had helped lots of people over the years. Others knew him from the newspaper column he wrote, called "Woods and Streams," which was published in five Montgomery County newspapers. So it was quite emotional at times as the people walked by the casket, sharing with me things Harry had done or said to them.

One, I shall never forget. A black man about 26 years old took my hand and, with tears running down his cheeks, told me he still had the fishing rod Harry gave him when he was 12 years old. (Harry took time during the summer day camp at Ambler High School to teach boys how to bait and cast a fishing rod. At the end of the six weeks of sharing and caring, Harry would give these boys the rod and reel they were practicing with — hoping the boys would go down along the Wissahickon Creek, rather than run in the streets. This fine young man had been one of those boys.)

The funeral service was held at the Ambler Church of the Brethren. The interment was at our Church of the Brethren Cemetery (original site of the Upper Dublin German Baptist meetinghouse), located between the Rose Hill Cemetery (originally a Lutheran burial ground) and the Rose Valley Cemetery (the Black burial ground). Each defined by a difference, which is quite a contrast for us Brethren. Aren't we supposed to love one another, no matter what color or denomination? (Well I say, "What a place to share our remains." I'm sure God put His blessings on the souls in those burial grounds the same as ours.)

Chapter 22

ON THE AUCTION BLOCK

Now I had to get on with my life. The business was put into my hands. I tried to be both Mother and Father to Scott, but I realized this was a terrible time for a boy to lose his father — he was just growing into a young man with many more needs than I could possibly give. Yet I strived to keep a family unit going.

Gail and Gary were very supportive, but they had their own lives to live. Their little girl, my first grandchild, was a godsend to me. Although I didn't have enough time to spend with her, I made Sundays our share time. My brother Glen, the last brother left from my immediate family, was retired and came to visit me almost every week. He had lots of time on his hands and he would also stop in at the store to see how things were going. His wife, Esther, was still working but planned to retire soon.

I was working twelve hours a day at the store. Harry had started these hours 9:00 a.m. to 9:00 p.m. years before, and I continued with them. I was to find out what it was like to be a businesswoman in a man's world. My first encounter came only about a month after Harry died.

I was in my office when this salesman came in whom we had known ever since we opened our business. He and his family had a multi-million-dollar business. He started telling me he "had the hots for me" (his own words). I thought at first he was kidding me, but when I stood up to go to my file cabinet to get his order, he grabbed me and pushed me up against the wall and tried to kiss me. I pushed him away and said, "What are you trying to do? Are you being funny?" He said, "No, I've had the hots for you for a long time and, since you no longer have a man, I thought you might be hurting and I could fill that need." I was shocked, hurt, and really mad, saying, "Get the hell out of my office, and don't you ever lay a foot in my store again!" My outcry of anger was very loud and Norm came running to my office and asked, "What's wrong?" I pushed this salesman at Norm and said, "Help him out of my store and NEVER order or buy anything from this man's Company again."

I started to cry. I grabbed my pocketbook and sweater and told Norm to close up the store and that I'd be in tomorrow morning. That was the first good cry I had since Harry died. I went home in tears, lay across my bed and wept until I was exhausted. (I must tell you I was never much of a crier. Even to this day, it takes a lot to make me cry. I work things out by working harder, or walking. When I get mad, I work out my frustrations by activities, but tears are not part of my makeup like a lot of women who can cry at the drop of a hat!) At the time, I also didn't want Scott to see me cry because I felt I had to be "tough" for him.

So my life as a single woman with a business and a teenage son was creating a new lifestyle for me — I became very business conscious, only to find out my business was in financial trouble. Before Harry died, I knew he was trying to borrow money from the bank. But I did not realize until later how much he owed some of the companies he dealt with. After about six months, I started getting calls from different businesses asking me where their payments were. Most of these companies knew by now that Harry had died and I was keeping the business going. However, they still had to be paid for their products which had been bought by Harry months before!

Remember I told you earlier, Harry would never let me see the books. Well, now I found out why Harry was so concerned about losing the business — he was $85,000 in debt! The economy was in a recession, banks were not lending money, and big businesses were demanding money as soon as products were delivered, with only a few days' grace on payment. If payment was not given in that amount of time an interest rate was charged.

So now I was caught up in a business bind. I had no one to talk to or share my frustrations with. My accountant was as helpful as he could be, but I needed money to make those payments. Since people were very cautious about buying, businesses were going bankrupt here and there at a rate unheard of since the Depression. I would go home at night with all these things on my mind and wonder what the next day would bring. I couldn't eat properly and started losing weight. I feared I would lose both the business and my home, but I decided to put things into God's hands. I had no other choice.

But becoming a Grandmom again brought great joy into my heart. On June 29, 1976, Megan Colleen McGinty came into this world. What a happy time for me and Scott; we now had another toy to play with, even though my time was limited with the business and this big, ten-room house which I took care of myself.

Remember my telling you about this Ed Simmers? Well, I received a phone call from him one evening when I came home from the store. He asked me if he could come to Ambler and spend a couple of days with Scott and me. I said, "You can come, but I won't have time to entertain you as I have to go to the store every day." He said, "THAT'S-OKAY-I'LL-SEE-YOU-SUN-DAY."

He got to our place Sunday evening. I noticed when he came in he had a suitcase and his briefcase (and I just assumed he still had his pistol in it that he always carried with him). After taking his suitcase up to his room, he came into the TV room where Scott and I were. He asked me if I had any time off the following week because he would like to talk to me. I said, "Wednesday afternoon I'm off."

When I came home Wednesday afternoon, I found Ed sitting at the dining room table with papers laid out in front of him. He looked up at me and said (with his "talker"), "YOUR-HUSBAND-SCREWED-ME-UP-WHEN-HE-DIED." I answered, "Screwed YOU up? What about ME?" Then he commenced to tell me that he had planned to will his farm to Harry, and now that Harry was gone, did I want it. Without hesitation I said, "No way do I want the farm. I don't have time to do what I have to do now without worrying about taking care of a farm a couple of hundred miles from here." He said, "DON'T-MAKE-UP-YOUR-MIND-NOW-BUT-THINK-ABOUT-IT-FOR-A-COUPLE-OF-MONTHS."

I asked him, "Did Harry know anything about this?" He said, "NO-I-WAS-GOING-TO-TELL-HIM-AFTER-I-HAD-THE-PAPERS-DRAWN-UP-BUT-NOW-WITH-HIS-DEATH-I-THOUGHT-YOU-MIGHT-WANT-IT." This was the first business encounter I had with this gentleman, but I was soon to be drawn into an affiliation that would turn my whole life around.

Although I have rarely been sick in my life, I was now starting to have pain in my lower right side. When I had a pap test, I told Doc Wiley. He examined me and found a small growth on an ovary, but he said we would watch it.

(I know now why I had open heart surgery a few years back. If I didn't have a good strong heart, I would probably never have been able to withstand the next few years without being an invalid, being bogged down to bed rest, which at that time was out of the question.)

I was quite aware that my business was in great financial trouble. There was not enough cash coming to pay the store rent, electricity bills, pay the two men working for me, pay my mortgage at home, plus utilities, and (most of all) keep up payments to the companies we owed. I kept all these problems to myself, hoping there would be a break in the economy and things would loosen up. But each day you would hear of another business going under. My mind was torn with such thoughts as, "I'll be next. I'll lose my home. What will I do?" (Please God, help me find an answer! If ever my Christian faith was being tested, it sure was now.)

Then I started to have trouble with Scott. He didn't want to come to the store after school but, instead, started to run the streets with a couple of boys who didn't have anything to do after school. We now began having confrontations and conflicts over discipline. I said, "If you don't come in and work, I'll not give you any spending money." He said, "That's okay." I was working twelve hours a day, coming home to make dinner and clean, and now I had a defiant son. (NOW was when I needed a man in the house.) I must say that this was the first time Scott had given me a rough time. He was 15 years old, and the loss and stress affected him too. He still was doing well in school, with passing grades, but he could have been on the Honor Roll.

One evening Ed Simmers called. He sensed that I was upset (I had just had another fuss with Scott) and asked, "WHAT'S-WRONG?" I said, "I'm so tired. Business is lousy. I think I'm going to go bankrupt." He said, "IS-IT-THAT-BAD?" and, in the next breath, asked if he could come visit for awhile.

I continued getting bad pains in my right side, which I was trying to fight off. Finally, one day after a sleepless night due to the pain, I made an appointment with Doc Wiley. After examining me he said, "You have to go to the hospital. The growth on your right ovary has enlarged and should be removed." I said, "I can't go to the hospital. I don't have time, plus I have no hospitalization." This was another thing Harry and I had argued about, his not having insurance or hospitalization. His answer was always "We'll take it from the business." But I was still paying on his hospital bill and now I had to go too! Boy, was my world tumbling down all around me! How could I handle all these things and keep my sanity?

February, 1977, I was in the hospital for seven days. When I was discharged, Gail came and stayed with me until I could go up and down stairs. The fellows at the store were really great. Helen Leadbeater took care of the books and, I found out later, she kept business calls from coming into our home.

One day, while I was home recuperating, the phone rang and a young boy's voice asked, "Is Scott there?" I answered, "He isn't home from school yet. Who's calling?" He replied, "None of your damn business," and hung up. Well, this took me by surprise. After a few more calls just as abrupt, I spoke with Gail and she said that she took some of those calls too and noticed they all started from 3:00 p.m. until 5:00 p.m. If Scott wasn't there, they would hang up and not say who they were.

Needless to say, this came to a showdown. I made a decision to send my son away for a few months to break this tie with these fellows who he was involved with. I made arrangements to send him to Florida to stay with my cousin, Walter Dailey, and his wife Myrtle. The night I sent Scott away, I cried all night. The next morning I was exhausted and drained.

Now I was at my lowest. My business was failing. My son was getting into trouble. I would probably lose everything I owned.

Besides Gail and Gary, my best friends were the Beisels. I didn't know which way to turn, so when I started sharing my problems with them, they would listen and try to advise me. But I had to make the final decisions.

While I was taking my shower to go down to the store for the first time after my surgery, I decided I was going to sell the store, pay all the debts, get another job, and get on with my life. Well, things just don't happen the way you think they should. It's like the prayers we make (and believe me, I was doing lots of praying right then). I didn't have any choice but to turn to God and ask for guidance, which at times seemed useless.

When I went into the store, Helen, Norm, and Glen were there to greet me. While I was recuperating, I would have to sign checks and give a few instructions as to what to do, but I will say they were all terrific through my whole ordeal. When I told them I had made up my mind to sell the business, they were shocked. I told them that I had talked to the accountant and shared with them the way the economy was. With all the threats from the companies we owed, it would take ten years to get on an even keel, and maybe not then.

I was going to be fifty years old and would have to work the next ten years just to scrape together a living, and besides, I didn't need the hassles from the public. We didn't own the building and rent was being raised every year. So my mind was made up.

Remember in the last chapter I told you about people's reactions when they heard about Harry's death. Well, on the Saturday morning of Harry's death I received a phone call from one of our customers by the name of Milton Wollman. He conveyed his condolences and said, "My family and I are going to Florida tomorrow for a week, but if you need a lawyer while I'm gone, call me night or day. I gave Norman my business card, and my secretary will relay any messages." I responded, "Thank you, but I don't see why I would need the services of a lawyer." (Boy, was I soon going to eat those words!)

A couple of days went by and I was still trying to make decisions on how was the best way to get rid of the store. I called several people who, at one time or another, said they would like a business like this. But when I contacted them, they wouldn't

205

"put their money where their mouth was" (so to speak). I asked Norm if he would like it. I offered to work a deal out with him to buy the stock and pay me so much a month — that way I would have an income until I knew what I was going to do with the rest of my life, and also get Scott graduated from high school and hopefully on to college. But Norm didn't want it, so I decided to have it auctioned off.

By this time I decided that I guess I did need a lawyer to help me do things right and also keep everything legal. Milton Wollman's name came to mind. I gave him a call at his Philadelphia office and his secretary took my name and phone number. About an hour later he called me and I told him what I intended to do with the Sportsman's Paradise store, and how much in debt I was, and how should I handle it?

Well, needless to say, this man and I spent quite a few hours together! He told me to put all my assets and debts together and decide from there. He wanted me to take Chapter 11 bankruptcy (reorganization to keep the business going), but I would not agree to that. He said, "I don't understand why you won't declare bankruptcy." I answered, "Because these bills have to be paid and I'm responsible for them."

Then he asked me, "Did you buy all this stuff?" I said, "No, Harry did." He said, "Then you are not responsible for this merchandise. Is your signature on the ordering slips?" I said, "No, Harry's is." Then he told me again, "Legally, you do not have to pay these bills." But I answered with, "I'm responsible for these bills because I'm his wife. I was raised that if a husband or wife had a bill, it had to be paid; it was their duty to abide by this rule. I'm a Brethren and our word is as good as a bond." He then took my hand and said, "I can see I'm not going to change your mind. I have never met anyone like you before."

By this time, Milt Wollman became part of my decision-making. I told him that no one I knew was interested in buying my store, so I had decided to auction the contents.

I contacted a reputable auctioneer by the name of Sanford Alderfer. He came to the store and looked over the merchandise and said he could sell it all in one day. And he would like to have it hauled to Skippack for the auction day. (Before he opened his large auction center in Hatfield, he rented the hall at the

Skippack Firehouse for these one-day auction sales.) This meant that everything in the store had to be transferred by truck to Skippack. So again, decisions, decisions. I went home that night with a heavy heart and asked God to help me make the right decision. Twenty-three years of my life with Sportsman's Paradise was going to be put behind me.

The next day I called Lansdale Transportation Company and made arrangements to have them pick up my merchandise on August 23rd. It took two large trucks to handle all the contents of the store. The fellows at the store and some friends helped load the trucks. It was very hard to watch my stock being tossed, and sometimes thrown, into these large vehicles. It took all day, since they also had to be unloaded and the contents displayed for the next day's auction, August 24, 1977.

Again I was exhausted that night, but had to go home and get rested for the next day's happenings. When I got to the auction site in the morning, people were already standing in line waiting for the auctioneer to open the doors. Norm and I went inside the hall, walked around looking at the contents, and noticed that some of our best rods and reels were missing — we couldn't find them. I assumed that someone had stolen them, either the movers, the night watchman, or the auctioneers' helpers, but we couldn't prove anything. That was the beginning of one of the saddest days of my life.

The auction started promptly at 10:00 a.m. It did not end until 11:00 p.m. that night. It started out rather well, getting good prices, but as the day progressed, people were getting restless. Also, there was still so much merchandise left that people got tired of waiting for the particular items they were interested in so they would leave. Fewer and fewer people were left to bid. By 6:00 p.m., my brother Glen said, "Ruth, I can't stand this; they're giving your stuff away." He went home very much discouraged with the auctioneers.

Norm left about 9:00 p.m. and said that it was killing him to see this merchandise go so cheap. Some things were being sold under cost! My precious friend, Quinn, stayed with me through the whole ordeal. I had to wait it out, even after realizing at some point I would not make enough money to pay the companies I owed!

The one thing that hurt me the most on that day was the personal appearance of a young man representing Girard Bank (where we had the store's account). He said to me, "As soon as you get paid this evening, I want the $10,000 you owe Girard before anyone else gets their money." I looked at him and said, "Are you telling me you can't wait until Monday morning? I was going to do that first thing."

When the auction ended, the auctioneer took his cut, and I was given a check for $27,000! That was it! That was all that was left of 23 years of sweat, tears, and decision-making. Yet those years were personally rewarding and a growing time in my life.

The Monday afternoon after the auction, I called Milt and told him what money I had left. The next evening he came to my home and I gave him a list of the companies I owed money. He sent letters to them explaining my circumstances. As a result, they were offered 25 cents on the dollar, so you know some of the companies just dropped their accounts and took what they could get. I closed the store on August 31, 1977.

I would like to inject here that Milt never sent me a bill for his services he rendered during the closing of the store. He knew I didn't have any money, even though I told him I would pay him when I started working.

The next few weeks after I closed the store, I got some letters in the mail with money in them. These folks told me at one time or another Harry had lent them money, and they wanted to pay their debt to Harry for his kind act! I found out from Helen Leadbeater later that Harry did this quite often. I will never know how many times he did this or how much he gave away, and am sure some money was never returned. But that was Harry — a terrific P.R. person, but a poor businessman!

Chapter 23

THE UNEXPECTED

I didn't know exactly what I was going to do, but I knew I had to go to work. Scott was 16 years old and had two more years of high school until he would graduate.

The phone rang one evening and it was Ed Simmers on the other end asking if he could come down. I said he could. Ed owned a car but never drove on the roadways; he had to be brought by one of his neighbors. On his farm he had a Jeep which he drove on his own property but never anywhere else. Remember he was blind in one eye, had poor vision in the other eye, plus he had bad legs, so even limited driving was quite a privilege for him.

When he arrived at my home, I noticed he had a large suitcase and a valise. And he was all dressed up in a suit and tie, and was clean shaven (which wasn't his cup of tea — he always had several days' growth of beard which made him look scraggly). After greetings and putting his suitcase into a bedroom, we started a conversation.

When we were talking awhile, Ed said, "YOU-HAD-A-LAW-YER-HELP-YOU-WITH-YOUR-STORE-DIDN'T-YOU?" I said, "Yes." He asked, "DID-YOU-TRUST-HIM-AND-WAS-HE-HONEST?" I said, "He was a godsend, and a very easy person to talk to." Ed asked me, "COULD-YOU-MAKE-AN-APPOINTMENT-WITH-YOUR-LAW-YER-NEXT-WEEK?" (This explained the large suitcase; he intended to stay awhile.)

A meeting was arranged with Milt at my home the following week. When Milt came to my house, I introduced him to Ed. It was awkward at first. Remember Ed talked through this mechanical gadget, his "talker", so I interpreted what Ed said at first and soon Milt could understand him. I excused myself and went up to the TV room with Scott. Milt left around 10:00 p.m.

Ed hired Milt as his lawyer. Ed's Maple Glen property was a triangle shape, with three main roads around it, so it had lots of potential for commercial development. Ed was having stores built on this property — the Maple Glen Shopping Center.

The next day, after his meeting with Milt, Ed told me he would like me to be the executrix of his estate. My reply was, "I don't know anything about real estate, and also I have to get a job!" (Remember before I told you Ed was going to make Harry his executor, but Harry died before he had papers drawn up — well, now he wanted me to take Harry's place.) I said that I would rather not; that he should get someone else. He said, "DON'T-MAKE-UP-YOUR-MIND-NOW-BUT-I'LL-CALL-YOU-IN-A-COUPLE-OF-WEEKS." Then he went home.

After he left, I found a check on my desk written to me for $1,000. I called Ed and said that I couldn't accept it. He said, "I'M-ONLY-TRYING-TO-HELP-YOU-AND-I-DON'T-WANT-YOU-TO-GO-TO-WORK." I said, "That's awfully nice of you, but I can't accept your money." He said a few choice words and made me promise to take it and pay him back some other time. Well, I owed him $10,000 for the down payment on this house; now another $1,000 added. I just couldn't see the light at the end of the tunnel.

Scott and I tried to maintain a living, plus Gail and family were very supportive. Scott got a part-time job at All Saints Hospital in Chestnut Hill (which later became the Abington Rehab Center), so he had his own spending money. I gave him Harry's station wagon which he used to go back and forth to work and school.

Again the phone rang and it was Ed. Could he come down for a couple of days; he had some business to attend to. Well his couple of days turned into a few weeks. Finally one day after Scott went to school, Ed said, "RUTH-COULD-I-STAY-WITH-YOU-AND-SCOTT-THIS-WINTER?" (It turned out that unbeknownst to me, and after we had bought this big house, Harry had told Ed that he could come and stay with us in the winter instead of being by himself on the farm. The house was big, with four bedrooms on the second floor, and three more rooms on the third floor. Remember, Ed was Harry's friend. Oh boy, now what do I do!) He said, "HOW-MUCH-ARE-YOUR-MONTHLY-BILLS?" I told him and he said, "I'LL-GIVE-YOU-A-THOUSAND-DOLLARS-A-MONTH-I-DON'T-WANT-YOU-TO-GO-TO-WORK."

If I accepted this arrangement, I'd be stuck with him — bad habits and all. And also, how much would he depend on me? I shared these thoughts with my brother Glen, and he said, "It sounds good if he doesn't want to own you." So, knowing that it had also been Harry's wish, I told Ed that we would try it for awhile.

Ed moved in with us full-time in the Fall of 1978. He was not the easiest person to get along with, but when he got into one of his moods, I'd go upstairs or take a ride. He and Scott got along pretty well, but I noticed that Ed sometimes picked on him. By this time, Ed had told me his whole life history — and it wasn't a very pleasant one.

One winter morning he said, "RUTH-I'D-LIKE-TO-GO-TO-FLORIDA. I-HAVE-NEVER-BEEN-OUT-OF-PENNSYLVANIA-EX-CEPT-TO-THE-JERSEY-SHORE." I said, "I can't take Scott out of school." He said, "GET-SOMEONE-TO-STAY-WITH-HIM." I told Glen and Esther about this and Glen said, "How about if we go along?" Well, it was settled. Soon Ed, Glen, Esther, and I were on our way to Florida in a new Lincoln Continental Ed had bought the week before. (This was my first new toy that I would be getting from Ed.)

The trip went well and we all had lots of fun. Ed knew something about every state, especially it's Civil War history. Even though he could barely see, he did a lot of reading all his life and retained everything he read. We visited some of our relatives and friends, but were glad to get home.

I have to share with you that before we went on this trip, I told Ed he would have to get some new clothes. We went shopping and I dressed him from head to toe — suits, ties, shirts, underwear, socks, and shoes. He got a big kick out of shopping and, most of all, was proud to be seen with this younger woman by his side. I didn't think too much about this until we were traveling, but I noticed him holding on to me when I helped him into and out of the car. He always wanted to open doors for me but I was too fast for him. One time he said, "YOU-KNOW-THAT'S-MY-JOB." I just laughed and shrugged it off.

I had been a widow for over a year, and I no longer wore my wedding ring. But it was not because I was ready to date again. (I have to confess that a couple of weeks after Harry died, I was sitting on the toilet twisting my wedding band around my finger. I got so mad that, as I walked back to the bedroom, I gave it a pitch and threw it at my jewelry box. I never found it. It probably went behind my dresser which was too heavy to move. I was mad at Harry for leaving me, and mad at God for taking him! And years later, when I moved, I never thought to look for it.)

When Ed moved in, he just became a part of our lives. He got a young couple to move in at the farm and look after it for him. He did not charge them any rent, but they paid their electricity. Their water was drawn from a well that he had put in. Leaving his farm was hard for him because he loved it, and he thought that's where he would spend his last years.

Now I was becoming involved to a small degree with Ed's financial standings, plus making appointments for him at Doctor's offices. He had to get new doctors in our area. He still had to have his throat checked twice a year at Geisinger Hospital where he had his voice box removed because of cancer (prior to this operation he had smoked two or three packs of cigarettes a day.) In addition to providing room and board for Ed, I was slowly getting entangled in an affiliation similar to a private secretary.

By that time, Ed was using the services of Milt Wollman quite a bit. He would call Milt for an appointment and Milt would always come to the house. I never had to take Ed into Philadelphia to Milt's office. When Milt came to the house, I would always go upstairs or go out somewhere, not knowing or caring what was being talked about.

One Sunday after church, Ed started asking me all about our church and what it stood for. I had lots of friends dropping in to see me and quite a few were church people. This impressed him. During this conversation I found out that he never belonged to any church. I was amazed and concerned. I asked, "Would you like to have my minister stop and see you?" He said, "I-THINK-I-MIGHT."

The following week I set a date with our minister, Jay Gibble, to come visit Ed. The visit went well. This surprised me because I thought Ed might give him a rough time (which he could do). Everything Ed asked, Jay answered with his professional expertise. When Jay left, Ed said, "YOU-KNOW,-I-LIKE-THAT-MAN-AND-WHAT-YOUR-CHURCH-STANDS-FOR."

A couple of weeks later Ed said, "CALL-YOUR-MINISTER. I-WOULD-LIKE-TO-BE-BAPTIZED." I asked, "Are you sure?" He answered, "YES." So it was arranged for Ed to be baptized in my living room in November 1978. Because of the hole in his throat, Ed could not be immersed in water, so he was baptized by sprinkling water on the head and laying on of hands by the minister and me, with the Deacons as witnesses. It was a very meaningful experience for Ed — he was now a member of the Church of the Brethren!

Chapter 24

A NEW DIRECTION

In 1979, I got an invitation to attend the Mock Family Reunion in Bedford County, Pennsylvania, my family's ancestral home. I hadn't been closely involved with this side of my family for a long time, except for my precious sister-in-law, Veron Rogers. After Alvin died, I would keep in touch with her by phone or visit her once a year. Glen and Esther had bought a mobile home in the same park where Veron lived, so they saw her more often than I did. They bought a mobile home there so they would have a place to stay on their monthly visits to see their son Barry at the School for Handicapped Children at Ebensburg, Pennsylvania.

When I received this Mock Reunion invitation, I decided to go. I hadn't gone anywhere by myself since Harry had died. I had taken Ed on some day trips to the Jersey shore, and the Florida trip, but that was all. I went to the reunion and stayed in Glen's mobile home.

I had a good time at the reunion seeing a lot of cousins and one uncle I hadn't seen since I was a little girl. Uncle Dorsey was Mother's brother, and his daughter and son-in-law had brought him with them from Michigan. We had lots of fun getting re-acquainted with one another. (He was 89 at the time; he lived to be 93.)

Near the end of the week I decided to go over the mountains to Windber, the coal mining town where I was born. It was a very depressed-looking place! Many buildings were boarded up, others very neglected. But houses that were still lived in were well kept and quite clean looking. I was glad Dad had made the decision to move down east years before. On my way home from Windber, after making a turn on Route 56 halfway down the mountain, I saw a sign on a tree which read "House For Sale With All Electric Heat".

A few days before this I was at a cousin's home and said, "Take me for a ride to look at some property you know that's for sale. Maybe I'll buy a few acres, if and when I sell my house. It might be a good investment, and also a great place to come to for vacations." He laughed and said, "You would never come back here anymore after all the years you've been down east."

I didn't see any acreage that turned me on, but then I remembered the sale sign on the tree. I told him about it and he said, "That sign has been on that tree for a long time." I said, "There has to be a home down in there." He said, "It's private property, so I wouldn't know." I said, "I took the phone number yesterday; we'll call when we get back."

Later I called the number and a man answered. I told him I had seen a sign on the tree and would he tell me about the home. He said, "Would you like to see it?" I met him the next day. As I was driving down the driveway, a spectacular view caught my eye. The gentleman was waiting for me outside the house; I introduced myself and we shook hands.

He took me inside, showed me around downstairs, and then upstairs (which had four bedrooms and a full bath). To say it was a "glorified log cabin" wouldn't do it justice. The two back bedrooms had large picture windows with a view down the mountain, and with an upstairs porch you could sit on. The downstairs had a living room with fireplace, a dining room, a small kitchen, and a powder room. From the dining room door, you could walk out onto a porch that ran the whole length of the house. All the downstairs had wooden beams. I fell in love with it! Mr. Kaufman had built this home for his retirement but his wife didn't like it, so he had put it up for sale. Three acres of property went with it, and he owned a couple hundred acres around it.

I told him I liked it but wasn't sure what I could do at the present time. We talked some more as he walked me to the car. During the conversation I told him that my parents were from that area, also that they were Brethren. He took my hand and said he was too; he went to the Walnut Grove Church of the

Brethren in Johnstown, Pennsylvania. I told him that I had been baptized by Rev. Paul Robinson Jr., whose father had been a minister there years before. Mr. Kaufman knew him very well. So this conversation proved fruitful. We shook hands again and I said, "I will go home and think about it and also share it with the family." As I was getting into the car I asked, "What price are you asking?" He said, "$40,000."

The next day I returned to my home in Ambler with all the good times and happenings to share with the family. When I told Ed about the house in Bedford, he said, "DO-YOU-LIKE-IT-THAT-MUCH?" I said, "Boy, you should see the view from the windows!"

The next day when Glen came to see me, I told my brother about it. I said, "I think I'm going to put my home up for sale. He said, "You mean you would move up there after all these years?" I told him that I had done a lot of thinking and sorting out things in my life while driving over that Pennsylvania Turnpike.

Scott would be graduating in June, and hopefully would go on to college. Scott and I had talked about college since he entered the eleventh grade. He had said he didn't want to go four years, but would like to go two years to the Montgomery County Community College just a few miles from Ambler. With this in mind, I had more decisions to make. Maybe, once in my life, I should think about me and what I wanted to do with my life. (God, guide me, please.)

On Glen's visit the following week, I was sharing how I felt and also about this property in Bedford. I said to him, "Would you like to see it?" So I phoned Mr. Kaufman and asked if we could see his property. The next day Glen, Ed, and I were on our way to Bedford. Mr. and Mrs. Kaufman were there to meet us.

Glen and Ed went inside and I said that I would like to walk around outside. Mr. Kaufman came with me, this time showing me the boundary lines to the property. I told him that I didn't have any money — I would have to sell my home and didn't know how long that might take. Also, I explained that I had a son who would be graduating and hopefully go on to college. Mr. Kaufman said, "We have a good college in Johnstown, an extension of the University of Pittsburgh."

We went back into the house and Ed was talking to Mrs. Kaufman. She was quite fascinated with Ed's "talker" and could understand him pretty well. Glen was standing on the porch, looking down the mountain. I asked, "What do you think?" He said, "It sure is nice, but do you want to live this far away from everybody?" I answered, "That's a decision I have to make."

When Glen and I went back inside, I noticed Ed talking to Mr. Kaufman, but didn't pay any attention. I went into the living room to Mrs. Kaufman and said, "This is a lovely home. How can you give it up?" She said that she didn't drive and, if they came here permanently, she would be stuck here. She loved to shop and take trips with girlfriends to Johnstown for lunch. The Kaufmans were in their early 70's — I imagine they had been thinking about selling for awhile.

As Glen and I were walking toward the car, I noticed Ed didn't come right away, and then I saw him and Mr. Kaufman shake hands. As they approached the car, I said to Mr. Kaufman, "I'm very much interested, so I guess I'll go home and put my house up for sale. If you sell this one in the meantime, I'll understand." He replied, "I'll wait — you're a good Brethren." I liked that. Time would tell!

Going home in the car, we were all rather quiet, each in his own thoughts. When we got home, I said to Glen, "I'm going to put my house up for sale." The next day I called Gail and told her I was going to sell my house and move to Bedford. She wasn't too happy about that. Neither was Scott. He said, "I'm not leaving my friends to go to some place I don't even know about!" I replied, "I don't know how long it will take to sell my house."

In June 1979, Scott (my baby son) graduated from high school. It was a nice ceremony, held at Temple University's Ambler Campus about a mile from where we lived. It was a hot night but a very memorable one for Gail and me. During the ceremony I was sharing with Gail that I felt bad that Scott didn't have his Dad to share this time of his life with him. We both had tears in our eyes as we watched Scott walk confidently past us with his diploma in hand. I had tried so hard to be both Mother and Father to him (and at the same time "spoiling him", according to Gail.)

Financially I was doing well enough, because Ed lived with us full-time and he paid me for the care. He didn't want me to work. Looking back, I think he liked having someone around and also he was from the Old School — "Women shouldn't work outside the home."

At the end of June, I called a real estate broker and made an appointment to have my home listed and appraised. I really liked this house; it was big and roomy with ten full-grown pine trees, nice shrubbery, and a winding driveway from the main street at the foot of the property. We had three acres to mow. Ed had brought his large mower down from the farm, and also a snow-blower. When Ed saw we needed something, he would always see that it was there for us to use. Scott and I always did the lawn, and I kept the inside of the home myself. About a year before, Ed also had one of his snowmobiles brought down so if we had any snow we could use it on our three acres plus the adjoining field.

One day not long afterward, the phone rang and it was my niece, Flora, on the other end. She was a beautician and was calling from the beauty shop. There was a lady who had just started coming to the beauty shop, and was looking for a place to stay during the week (going home over the weekends) and said she would rather stay in a private home than in a motel. Flora had told her, "My Aunt Ruth has a big home with extra bedrooms. Let me call her!" I told her to send this lady around. Maybe it would be nice to have another woman in the house.

When she stopped in, we sat in the kitchen and talked, sizing each other up. We got along well enough at this short meeting, so I showed her around my house and took her upstairs to the third floor. I showed her the room I would give her. I said, "If you are interested, I'll paint and put curtains up." She said that she would let me know the following week.

Well, needless to say, we had a new person — Reggie Hepner — to share our home. She was a registered nurse and was hired by the State of Pennsylvania to inspect and observe nursing homes to see that they kept up with the health codes, and if people in the homes were clean and taken care of properly.

We became good friends. Her husband, Will, had just retired from the Army with the rank of General. They were originally from Virginia, so after retiring he went home (so to speak) to look for a house while Reggie had another year to work until she could retire too. I didn't have to cook for her. She ate before she came home at night or she would make her own dinner. I gave her room in the refrigerator for herself. She got up early in the morning, made coffee and toast, and then went on her way. So it was not an inconvenience to have her stay with us.

Scott was still at home, working the summer at the hospital, and getting ready for college in the Fall.

Remember my telling you when we were looking at the home in Bedford, Ed was talking to Mr. Kaufman? Well, Ed wrote a check to the Kaufmans for $5,000 to hold the property, knowing I would probably be selling my home in the future. Also, he liked it too! They wrote the agreement on the back of an envelope and Ed signed it! With a verbal agreement, Ed would send $500 a month until the transaction could take place. Again Ed used his "smarts" to entice these people into this position. I didn't know anything about this until it came time to write Ed's checks for the month. He said, "NOW-I-WANT-YOU-TO-SEND-A-CHECK-TO-KAUFMAN-FOR-FIVE-HUNDRED-DOL-LARS." When I questioned him, he then told me what he had done.

Oh my gosh! What am I going to do now? I was thinking if I sold my home, I would move to Bedford with Scott and make a new life for ourselves. I was hoping that I could talk Ed into going into one of the fine retirement homes in our area. He was starting to have trouble walking and, also, it was getting harder for him to breathe. I noticed he was coughing more often and did a lot of sleeping during the day.

When I approached him about going into a retirement home, he threw his "talker" across the table and mouthed, "ARE-YOU-TRYING-TO-GET-RID-OF-ME?" We never had too many disagreements, but if we did, I would walk away. I tried to explain to him that maybe soon I wouldn't be able to take care of him and he should be where he would get care twenty-four hours a day. He didn't talk too much for a couple of days.

After those few days, I was taking the dishes from the table when he took my hand and said, "SIT-DOWN. I-WANT-TO-TALK-TO-YOU. I-DON'T-KNOW-HOW-LONG-I'M-GOING-TO-LIVE. IF-

I-GET-DOWN-SICK-I-WANT-TO-STAY-HERE. YOU-CAN-HIRE-NURSES-TO-TAKE-CARE-OF-ME. I-WOULD-NOT-WANT-YOU-TO-WALK-AFTER-ME." I said, "Let's not worry about it now but wait and see what happens."

Chapter 25

MORE GOODBYES

In October of 1979, Ed asked to be taken up to his farm for a couple of days, to be driven by a friend of his. He wanted to check on it and also see how the new family was taking care of things. He had to get rid of the first caretakers — they had separated and the woman was trying to keep things going by herself but couldn't, so Ed let them go. A neighbor told Ed about this other couple, and Ed had moved them in a few months before. Now he wanted to see how things looked, plus October is a beautiful time at the mountains. He did not realize that this would be the last time to see this beautiful farm. (Or maybe he had an intuition. Who knows?) When he returned to Ambler, he seemed quite content and happy.

Remember, Ed was doing very well financially by this time. He was getting a good pension from the Postal Department, plus some rental income from his commercial property at Maple Glen. Sometimes he would say to me, "SHOULD-I-GET-THIS?" I would say, "It's your money. Get whatever you want." Here was a man who never had much all his life; now he could get whatever he wanted, but his age and poor health were against him. That's why I think when he saw what we needed, or thought I would like to have, he would get it. I remember him looking at an Eddie Bauer Catalog and wondering if he should get a beautiful two-piece down jacket and pants set — it cost $500. I said, "Go ahead and order it; you worked hard for your money, you deserve it." He ordered a lot of things through the catalogs. Remember, he didn't drive a car and living on a farm he didn't get to shop in stores too often, so this became a pastime — looking through catalogs and magazines of all sorts.

I would like to inject at this time, when Ed lived on the farm he had it completely furnished with his parents' antiques and some that he had bought himself. He liked nice things. He had quite a few guns and pistols which he had bought from Harry over the years. He had one room full of all kinds of gun reloading equipment, shells, binoculars, and hunting equipment worth thousands of dollars which he had accumulated. He also had a large collection of records, from classical to cowboy music, and readings from such greats as Will Rogers and Edward R. Murrow narrating historical events, and many more prominent orators. He was a self-educated man. I remember one day I was sitting at the table writing checks and adding some figures on paper when he said, "WHY-DO-YOU-ADD-LIKE-THAT? IT-TAKES-TOO-LONG." He could run his fingers down a column without marking numbers you add and put it on paper before I was halfway through. He was very sharp with figures. That's why he was on top of everything when he had the stores built on his property.

By November 1979, the weather was getting colder and I was getting ready for Thanksgiving. We had a few people look at my house, but no takers. I was wondering how soon we might be leaving "Rose Hill". I really loved this old house, but it was too large and with all the lawn to be cut, it was becoming a chore.

I invited Gail, Gary, and their girls for Thanksgiving dinner which was fun for all of us. I had lots of room and the girls loved to run up the front stairs and down the back stairs, off Scott's bedroom. I have to inject at this time about Megan's antics. Ed had his "talker" and when he wasn't using it, he would lay it on the table. Whenever Megan saw it, she would grab it and run away with it to tease him. Also, she would try to put it into her mouth to try and talk through it. Ed never was around children very much. He got a big kick out of them sometimes, but if they got too noisy, he would go up to his room.

With Thanksgiving out of the way, we started to think about Christmas. Again, it was catalog time for Ed. He saw this London Fog all-weather coat for women and said, "YOU'D-LOOK-GOOD-IN-THIS. WHAT-SIZE-DO-YOU-WEAR?" Well, that was my Christmas gift from him. He ordered a chamois shirt for Scott and some things for himself.

Ed never had much of a family, so Christmas wasn't played up too much for him as a kid. And also there was a Depression going on. His parents had a general store and Post Office at Maple Glen, which was his homestead. In those days two and three generations lived together which was the thing to do, so businesses were automatically handed down from one generation to the other. Remember Ed was a third generation Postmaster, and he liked the Post Office. He said it was a challenge to him, plus he got to meet and know lots of people. Some people liked him and some didn't. He was hard to get close to because he didn't trust most people. I think that went back to his childhood when his Mother protected him because of his ailments.

We were getting ready for Christmas, one day I said, "I'm going to get a Christmas tree." Ed said, "I'LL-GO-WITH-YOU." We went to this nursery off Stump Road and found a beautiful eight-foot Douglas fir. It cost $30. I thought it was too much, but Ed said, "GET-IT. IT-ONLY-HAPPENS-ONCE-A-YEAR-ANYWAY-I-HAVEN'T-HAD-A-TREE-SINCE-I-WAS-A-KID." That tree was beautiful in our 18 x 30 foot living room. We put it into a corner facing the front door. Our home sat high, overlooking homes and the street below. We had a nice setting. The living room was great for entertaining.

Our Christmas went well, but it still was hard without Harry. This was our second Christmas without him. I was still involved in church choir, but was no longer teaching Sunday School, which I had to give up when Harry got sick.

After Christmas, I noticed that Ed was getting tired more quickly, his coloring was yellowish, and his breathing harder. He would get mad very quickly, and was short with me sometimes, and especially with Scott. He was also doing much more sleeping in his chair. I decided to make an appointment with his doctor, but Ed got too sick before the appointment time. On January 4, 1980, Ed was put into Chestnut Hill Hospital. He had trouble breathing. Also, his cancer was all through him. The doctor told me it was just a matter of time. (So soon! What do I do now but wait?)

Also in the first week of January, my brother Glen was taken to North Penn Hospital with severe pains in his stomach. He was given all kinds of tests, but they did not know what was wrong with him. I was running back and forth from one hospital to the other. What a time!

After Ed's seventh day in the hospital, the doctor said that there was nothing more they could do. He just needed bedrest. With Ed's persistence, I asked the doctor if he could come home. The doctor said, "If you have someone to take care of him, I don't see why not." So I brought Ed home, not knowing for sure what was in store for me. Glen was still in the hospital.

Remember I told you earlier about Reggie living with us? (Whether it was coincidence or providence, I needed her nursing experience and advice now more than ever.) I brought Ed home, and when Reggie came home, she would stop in his room and check him out and talk with him awhile. She would also tell me to go see my brother.

I would help Ed sit on the edge of the bed and bathe him from a basin. Then I would go out of the room while he washed his privates. When he was finished, I would take the basin away and empty it in the bathroom. I was bringing all Ed's meals up to him. I had a bell by his bed. If I was downstairs doing something, I could hear it. Also, Ed could "click his tongue" if he didn't want to use the "talker", and by this time he was doing quite a bit of clicking.

The next night when Reggie came home, I told her Ed hadn't gotten out of bed all day except to go to the toilet, which was a port-a-pot I rented from the drugstore and put next to his bed. Reggie asked me if I was going to see my brother and I said, "I don't know if I should." She said, "Go ahead. I'll look in on him." (God bless her.) Her room was above his, so it wasn't far away. The stairway to the third floor was wide with a large landing which I had made into a sitting room for Reggie. It was quite comfy, and this gave her a place to read and do her paperwork at night before she went to bed.

On my way to North Penn Hospital to see Glen, I was thinking to myself and wondering how long I would be able to take care of Ed.

When I went to the ICU, my brother wasn't there. I asked the nurse where he was and she said they had moved him to a semi-private room that afternoon. I thought, "Great, he's getting better! I guess they found out what was wrong with him." I walked into the room. He was glad to see me. I kissed him and said, "Boy, you gave me a scare!" His reply, "Don't stand in front of the window — I want to look out." He had been in Intensive Care so long with no view, he longed to look outside.

As we were talking, Esther and Carol came in. I said, "Since you're here, I'll go home." I kissed Glen goodbye and said, "I'll see you tomorrow night." I went home. Back home, Scott was in the TV room. We talked a few minutes and then I went to Ed's room and asked him if he wanted anything. He shook his head, no.

Reggie came to the TV room as I came out of my bedroom. I had just put on my pajamas and was getting ready to settle down for the night. She said, "Ed didn't want to take his medicine, so I didn't fight him." I said, "I'll check on him after awhile. Maybe he'll take it for me." Ed was getting quite contrary. That's why I was thinking on the way to the hospital how long could I handle him myself.

About 10:00 p.m., Reggie said she was going upstairs. She looked in at Ed and said, "See you tomorrow, Ed!" I went into the TV room with Scott, then at 11:00 p.m. I said, "I'm going to check on Ed and give him his medicine and go to bed." When I went to Ed's bedside with water and pills, he shook his head and pushed my hands away. He mouthed these words, "I'M-DYING. NO-PILLS." I looked at him and said, "Not tonight, I don't have time." (Every time he said he was going to die, I would repeat those words — I said them quite a few times over the past year.)

I didn't force him to take his medicine. I sat on the edge of his bed and told him if he didn't feel better, maybe I should call the doctor tomorrow. I said, "Goodnight; I'm next door, if you want me, click."

I fell asleep but woke up about 3:00 a.m. (when someone is sick you never sleep well, one ear is always waiting for a call in the night). I went into Ed's room and bent over him to hear him breathe. No sound. I put my fingers on his neck — no pulse, nothing. He was dead. My heart started pounding. I called to Reggie and she came running down the steps, took his pulse, and said, "He's gone." Being a nurse, I knew she had been through experiences like this before. She said, "I didn't think he would last long when he refused his medicine tonight. You better call the doctor; he'll have to pronounce him dead." The doctor was there within an hour. He called the undertaker for me — my good friend, Anton Urban.

The phone rang about 7:00 a.m. It was my niece, Carol Reimel, saying, "I have some bad news — Daddy died this morning at 5:00 a.m." (Oh my gosh, what next?) I told her about Ed. Ed and Glen died about three hours apart on January 17, 1980, which was also Carol's birthday. I told her to make arrangements with Esther and call me back later that day. I told Anton about Glen's death and said, "Ed doesn't have any relatives except a girl cousin. Could you wait to set the funeral arrangements?" I called Milt Wollman a few hours after Ed died to let him know. He asked, "Do you need any help to make arrangements?" I said, "I can handle it." He said, "Let me know the time for the funeral and I'll be there."

Later that Thursday afternoon, Carol called me and said that Glen would be laid out Monday evening, with the funeral on Tuesday, and he would be laid to rest at Whitemarsh Cemetery. When I took Ed's clothes to the undertaker's and told him about the arrangements for Glen, he asked, "Is Saturday too soon to bury Ed?" I said that it was okay with me. He had put the death notice in the paper, which gave people time to read and acknowledge it.

My family, a girl cousin, Milt, and a few friends were all Ed had. So the funeral was small. Ed was buried at the Rose Hill Cemetery next to his parents. He had lived 72 years. I had a funeral luncheon at my home after we came from the cemetery.

At the luncheon, Milt asked if I would have time to talk to him later. After everyone else left, Milt and I went into the living room. He said, "You know, I made quite a few visits here this past year. Ed earmarked his estate to go to charity eventually, but he named you executrix, so you will get an income from managing the estate as long as you live." I couldn't believe what I was hearing, and said, "I had no idea he was doing that for me. Why didn't he tell me?" Milt said, "That was his way of thanking you for what you had done for him these last few years of his life. He also told me he couldn't trust anyone else with his property and money!" (Wow, I had to let this sink in!) Milt ended with, "I'll call you next week and give you more details."

Attending Glen's viewing on Monday evening was very emotional for me. My last brother was gone — now I was the last one left of the John Rogers family. Glen had retired a few years before, so this gave him quite a bit of free time. He did not have any hobbies, so he had visited me almost every Wednesday afternoon. We grew closer than we had ever been in our lives, so his death was quite a deep hurt in my life. (Now what was God doing to me!)

Just three days before, I had laid Ed to rest. Now on Tuesday I watched as Glen was laid to rest — my last, precious brother. Glen had been a manager for Clemens Markets for years, so it was a large funeral. A lot of people knew him. Relatives had gathered, plus people from far and near — so there was lots of sharing and tears.

My house was really big now for only Scott and me. (Reggie stayed on for awhile — then one weekend when she was driving home to Virginia she was hit head-on by a truck that had crossed the median strip. She was almost killed, suffering broken bones from head to toe, and spent a year in the hospital. But she recovered. She had to retire sooner than she wanted to.)

At the end of January my phone rang, and it was the real estate lady saying that she would like to show my home to someone. I said, "Okay!" The next day she brought this gentleman over. I knew that whenever realtors bring people to show your house, they would rather not have the owner there, so I left. One day later, I got a phone call from the realtor saying she had a buyer for my house. Boy, was I excited!

I called Milt and he said, "Have her draw up the papers but don't sign anything until I see it." (Can you believe it? Only a few weeks after two funerals, my house sold — that meant I was free to move to Bedford and start a new life! Thank you, God, for watching over me — you're not such a bad guy after all! All my heartaches can fade away; I have something new to look forward to. I will be getting a nice monthly income from Ed's estate, plus widow's pension. My life is making a complete turnaround. Thank you, dear God, thank you!)

When it came time to sign the final agreement for the sale of my property, Milt asked, "How old are you?" I said, "Fifty-four." He said, "When will you be fifty-five?" I said, "September 10." He said, "They just passed a law that you can get a tax break on the sale of a home — a one-time deal; so if you want to make the settlement, make it after your fifty-fifth birthday." I called the realtor and told her about this and she said that she would ask the buyer for an extension. He agreed, so settlement was set for September 15, 1980.

The first week of February 1980, I called the Kaufmans at Bedford and told them my house had sold and that September 15 was the settlement date. This gave them time to enjoy their home for another summer, with over six months to remove their furniture.

My life became more relaxed and I had more time to spend with Scott and my two precious granddaughters. Megan was going on 3, and Kelly, 6. I would keep them some days for Gail. My yard was big, so they had lots of room to run and play. I would give them each a bucket of water and a paintbrush and they would pretend they were painting my house. (Oh, what joy grandkids are! I can love them, and spoil them; then take them home!)

My sister-in-law, Esther, had been married to Glen for thirty-four years when he died. This was a great loss for her, even though Carol and the grandkids lived nearby. Barry was still many miles away at the School for Handicapped Children in Ebensburg, Pennsylvania. I could tell she was having a hard time getting over Glen's death.

After seeing her one evening, I went home and started thinking about what she and I had just gone through a couple of months before. I thought, "Wouldn't it be nice if we could get away for a couple of weeks?" A few days later I called her and suggested it to her. She said, "Boy, would I like that! But I don't know if I can get off work." Before the week was out she called and said, "When do you want to go?" We started making plans and decided the second week in March we would go off for two weeks to Florida to visit our cousins, Walter and Myrtle Dailey.

Chapter 26

TESTAMENT

By 1980, I had been a widow for five years. I had accepted a few dates now and then, but nothing serious. I made up my mind when Harry died that I would get Scott raised before I made a commitment to anyone else. And then again, maybe I might not find anyone who would want me!

One day when I was driving home from shopping for things for my upcoming Florida trip with Esther, I noticed this nice maroon car following me up my winding driveway. As I got out of the car, I noticed this man walking towards me. He said, "Hi, Mrs. Stokes." I paused, then realized who it was, and replied, "Hi, Mr. Lewis!" He was one of my customers from the store.

He asked, "May I help you carry some of your packages for you?" He was dressed in sport clothes, and I remembered that he always came into the store neatly dressed, but smelling faintly of liquor, and usually had a big cigar in his mouth. I told him to sit down and offered him a cup of coffee. He said, "No thanks."

He said that he was sorry to hear about Harry, and that his wife had just died in February. I said that I was sorry too (although I didn't know her). I asked, "How did you know where I lived?" He said that he had been in Ambler the day before and saw me drive by, so he thought he would give me a call. But when he had tried to call me, my phone number wasn't in the book. (People were still calling me about the store, even after it had closed, so I had it changed to an unlisted number.) He said when he saw me pull into this driveway, he followed me up the hill to my house.

Then I asked, "Would you like a drink?" and he said, "I thought you would never ask." I made him a highball, and made a cup of tea for myself. (I would like to inject here that Harry and I never were drinkers — from my being raised in a Brethren home, and Harry becoming a Brethren. Also, Harry didn't like the taste of alcohol, although I liked wine.)

Thinking back to the weeks just after Harry died, my grief was so strong that I was tempted to dull it with alcohol. I would come home from the store tired and exhausted, and would take a glass of wine to relax me. Sometimes I would take a second glass. Sadly, one evening I was about to pour the third glass when I thought to myself, "What am I DOING? Am I going to use this as a crutch? Maybe I'll get to depend on it!" That was the last time I drank by myself. (I would have a drink once in awhile, but did not make a habit of it. If I entertained for dinner, I would serve wine.)

When I handed Mr. Lewis his drink, I said, "Let's go into the living room." I can still see him sitting on my antique settee. He looked so small and forlorn. We made small talk. Then he said, "Do you date? Are you dating anyone now? If not, would you go out to dinner with me Saturday night? I'm so darn lonely!" (This is another story I'll write another time!)

It took me almost fifteen years from the time I started writing this book's first chapter to arrive at this last chapter. And now, still being a Mother, I want to hand out some advice to my precious children, Gail and Scott. Rev. Lynn Leavenworth said that, back in earlier days, people used to write their "Last Will and Testament." The will was for the disposition of their earthly goods, and the testament was a summation of what they had learned from life and wanted to pass on. Well, my will is at the lawyer's office but here, dear children, is my testament:

We must cherish our yesterdays but never carry them as a burden into the future. Each generation must take nourishment from the other and give knowledge to the one that comes after. Even if the past was not kind to you, take time to remember. Make an enduring and loving home for your children's memories, then leave them to build on that foundation their own home of the future. Today is yesterday's tomorrow.

Isn't life interesting!

Your mother,

Ruthie

**Many blessings to my two precious children—
Gail and Scott**

Appendix

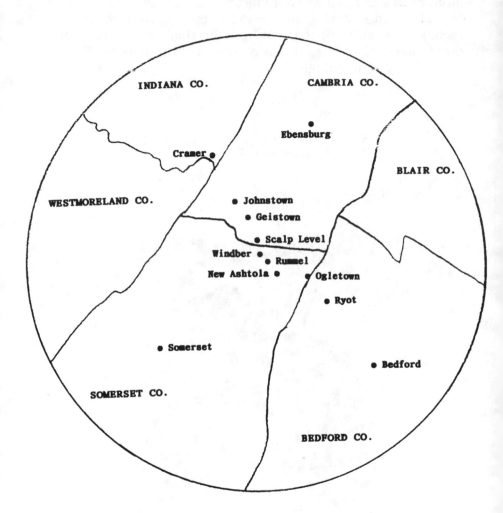

Western Pennsylvania

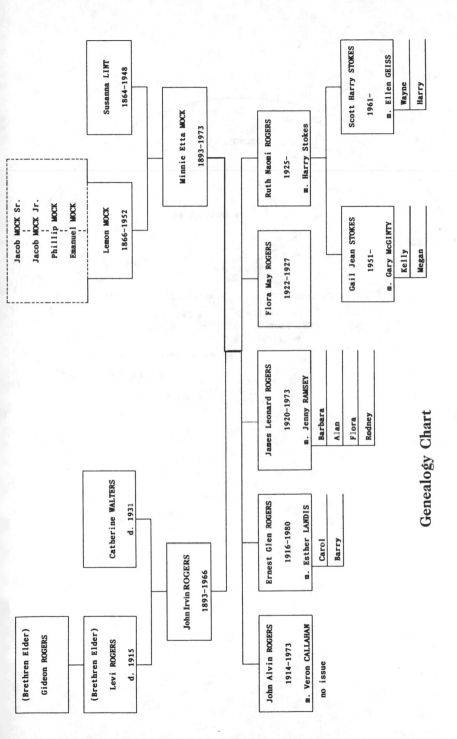

Genealogy Chart

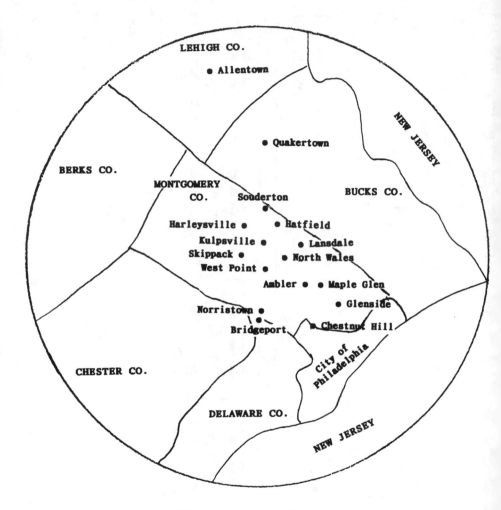

Eastern Pennsylvania

234

Index

236

Church of the Brethren Home Page

http://www.tgx.com/cob

To order additional copies of

Ruthie, Brethren Girl

Please send $15.00* (includes shipping &
any applicable tax) to:

Ruth R. Stokes
12 Bentwood Circle
Harleysville, PA 19438

*Quantity Discounts Available

E-mail: MizRuthie@aol.com